The
DeNIM
DIARIES

a memoir

Laurie Boyle Crompton

 ZEST BOOKS
MINNEAPOLIS

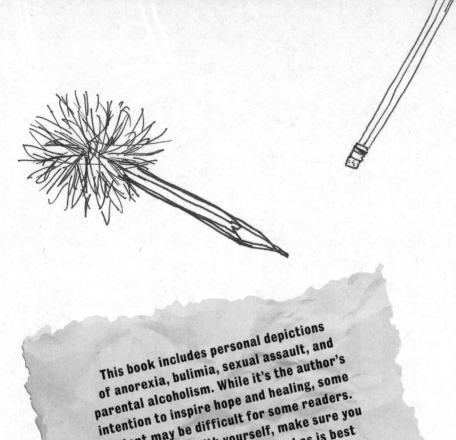

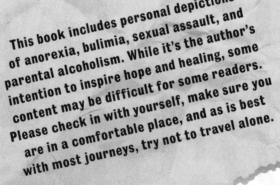

This book includes personal depictions of anorexia, bulimia, sexual assault, and parental alcoholism. While it's the author's intention to inspire hope and healing, some content may be difficult for some readers. Please check in with yourself, make sure you are in a comfortable place, and as is best with most journeys, try not to travel alone.

Table of Contents

Author's Note

John Hughes released his legendary classic, *Sixteen Candles*, the year I turned sixteen.

Sixteen Candles

The movie opens with a shot of Molly Ringwald sitting at her bedroom vanity as she assesses her image in the mirror. That was me. Every single day I studied my reflection. Judged my appearance. Except that while Molly wished for an additional "four inches of bod," I needed to be smaller. Thinner. *Always less.*

It was the mid-1980s, and I wore my high-waisted jeans so tight I had to lay back on the bed and hook a wire hanger through the zipper to force the fly closed. This was before denim knew the forgiveness of stretch, and so I would penguin about my high school's hallways, my stride restricted by my dark blue butt tourniquet. Each night it took hours for the red map of seams imprinted on the lower half of my body to fade.

An academic slacker, I spent more time studying fashion magazines than any textbook. I had to bluff my way through the periodic table of elements but never missed a single issue of *Glamour*. Obviously, my very first diet was a clichéd attempt to look like a fashion model.

By the time I turned sweet sixteen—giggling through *Sixteen Candles* and obsessed with boys—I had developed a not-so-sweet eating disorder.

Since that time, we've all come to see the underlying racism and rapeyness in that film, yet our culture of thinness has grown even more toxic. By current standards, that first pack of supermodels I tried to emulate back in the '80s would be considered plus-sized. Also in the 1980s, digital retouching was new, and its kung fu was weak. Today, flawlessness has been driven to new levels of aspirational fiction. We are living in a world where half of all six-year-old girls believe they're too fat, and holy shit, they're only six.

As a teenager, I swallowed the lie that fat is fundamentally loathsome, aesthetically ugly, and morally evil. I made myself hostage to the back-and-forth number on my bathroom scale. I despised my belly and thighs and especially my butt—I'm talking, I wasted a ridiculous amount of my young adult life focused on hating the size of my own ass.

My body-hatred led me to desperation, but even at my worst, I found flickers of hope. As the torch-wielding lady on the Columbia Pictures logo got thinner and thinner, the Statue of Liberty's mid-'80s makeover changed only one aspect of her appearance. She got a new torch.

So now I'm here to proclaim, "Give me your brainwashed, self-loathing masses yearning to breathe Spanx-free!" And you might want to grab a fat neon scrunchie and an oversized set of shoulder pads, because we're about to moonwalk back to the 1980s in all its material-girls-just-wanna-have-fun glory.

My hope is that by sharing my story with a *mortifying* level of honesty, you will see that you and your uniquely *you*-sized ass are not alone. No matter what shape. No matter what size. Every rear end is worthy of love.

This book is my torch.
May you, dear reader,
discover the FREEDOM
to **love yer butt!**

XO
Laurie

Prologue

Mirror Pep Talk, circa 1988

Good morning, sunshine.
Look me straight in the eye.
I'm just checking in to ask: what is
the matter with you?
You are such an utter embarrassment
with that accursed ass of yours.
It's a very simple concept, dear:
Stop with all the eating already.

Time to focus up.
You came to conquer New York City?
Let's look at all the ways you are failing.
No job. No car. And everybody whispering
"What's up with that blond chick?"
That's you.
What the hell is up with *you*?

Throwing up isn't working anymore.
Your bloated body is disgusting,
not to mention, I suspect,
puking your own blood is not a very good sign.
But even worse, you will remain
hopelessly   humongous
if you don't just stop with all this damn
EATING.

One thing I think we can agree on:
you are *never*
touching laxatives again.

Eating disorders are a big tub o' laughs
until that one day when
you crap your jeans.

One / The Girl Who Wants Too Much

Rewind, circa 1968

My grandfather presses to have me "taken care of"
as I sit stubbornly in his teenage daughter's womb
a wild weed threatening all her
                beautiful promise.

Grandfather knows what to do:
a quick trip to Mexico,
a brief procedure
and all will be
fixed
dealt with.

I will be nothing.

But Mom refuses.
Calls off the contract hit
makes a husband of the
handsome lout
who knocked her up. My dad.
Barely twenty
but so very in love as he
moves us 400 miles deep into Pennsylvania,
away from New York
and from everyone's
bright and shining dreams
for her.

The Way

Their marriage is *bumpy.*
I'm nearly five before they
find Jesus
are *born again*
and begin to pray and pray
and pray
for a baby because

babies are a blessing now.

We camp outdoors with
other Jesus freaks
read from the Hippie Bible
go to Jesus festivals
where all dance and sing
together
like we're at Woodstock.

I made Mom and Dad miss
their Woodstock
with my ~~unfortunate~~
~~unplanned~~
unprayed-for arrival.

I delight in the open air celebration,
reckless joy racing
across the field
swirling in the air with
Christian folk songs.
Hand-painted banners announce
> *JESUS IS ALIVE!*
I plunge right in. My child-voice
shouting with the crowd
we came to
> *Praise the Lord!*
Jesus fills me
> from the heart outward
> love settles delicious on my skin
> and I am whole.

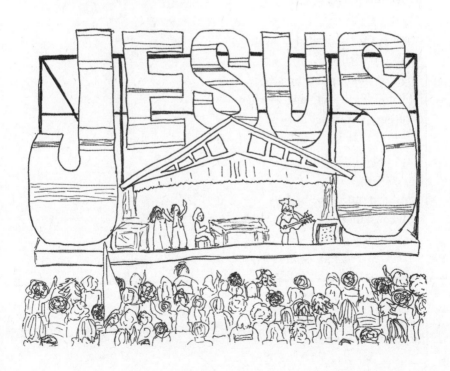

Plan B

Finally
praying pays off and
precious Cara
arrives.
The most beautiful Gerber Girl
with wise blue eyes that take in
everything.
And because we have prayed
so hard
eighteen months later
extra overflow blessing
baby Christopher,
prized BOY with
the best bald head
perfect for hugging.

Mom is a three-headed creature,
a baby on each side,
tiny fists holding soft unwashed hair
fat baby feet kicking one another
dividing our mother in two.

Cara and Christopher
bring ~~chaos~~ joy
transform our peaceful days
with constant noise
    giggles, wails
      toys that talk and honk!
and constant smells.
    Diaper check!
I play proud errand girl,
racing in with wipes

when Mom shouts,
"Oh my God—poop up to the neck!"
Hold my nose hauling
overburdened diapers outside,
fetch teethers and blankies,
climb inside cribs and playpens,
make up zany stories,
read picture books using all the voices.
The resident goofball entertainer,
I'm told I am the best big sister ever
which is an easy thing
since I love my job.

Plan B, Part 2

Mom won
a modeling contest in high school
for free lessons
at Barbizon Modeling School
in New York City.
Mom was supposed to be
a chic metropolitan model.
Not just some mom
living in the sticks with
three ragamuffin kids
constant static in our hair
and a mustached mate
with movie star looks who
drinks too much
     comes home late
doesn't drink too much
     comes home on time
       with magic and laughter
       and a borrowed pet ferret or
       a plump toad saved from the road

and sometimes Dad drinks so much
is so much fun
     he forgets to come home at all.

But Mom is great at being Mom.
Bakes brown bread as we twirl
to crackling records.
Sets our minds afire for reading.
Everyone is rich at the library!
Sings her bright Jesus songs,
loudly and out of tune
and with all her heart.

Our home is stocked with cats
despite Mom's wicked allergy:
she reciprocates feline affection
with red, watery eyes.

A displaced New Yorker,
embracing the quirks
of country life.

She paints and sews
mashes meaty strawberries
into jam
laughs when
the neighbors whisper
about her and Dad being
"those hippies" from New York
slowly tightening the elastic band
on her sarcasm,
sliding acidic asides
beneath her breath.

She shines lemon-scented daylight
into our childhood.
We are without a doubt
        the life Mom loves.
But we are not
        the life Mom planned.

Western Pennsylvania

My insides crave
the outside.
Linked with nature, I am
"that weird girl" who doesn't quite fit in
sitting in a tree,
sliding hands across rough bark
gripping branches, hugging trunks
as the trees and I listen
together for a whisper from Jesus who
loves me, loves me, yes,
Jesus loves me.

Walking barefoot across our green hill,
over clover and cheerful dandelions,
I step on an average of
six unlucky bees per summer.

Mom, removing
yet another thick stinger
from my reddened heel,
suggests with frustration,
"Shoes perhaps??"
But the hot prick
and lingering swollen itch
cannot eclipse
soft, cool grass
against bare soles.

Dreamer

According to the rainbow poster
on the door of our art room,
all children are artists.
The trick is in the not forgetting
as we grow up.

I solemnly swear
         I will never forget.
I am an artist.

Love to daydream for long
cat stretches of time.
My teachers all hate this, want me to click
back to their boring station.
Except the art teacher
who praises what comes out:
         a pouting papier-mâché mask
         a picture garden of watercolors
         a purring charcoal drawing.
The school hallways, a gallery
promoting my efforts, proof I'm here
if not always present,
as I curl into my warm imagination.

I am watching
patiently because
I was made
for something special.
I don't know when or
from where or even
what it is
but I will recognize it
when it comes.

Road Trip

We live in Butler, PA,
but New York is "back home."
Each school break
with Gran Torino loaded
we sit three across
the tan back seat
with one holy, pillow-sized bag.
Orange cheese puffs
to ease the dull pain
of nothing to do.

The puffs don't last
to Route 80.

I lead Cara and Christopher
bickering thorough the seven-hour
smelly disheveled road trip
on a bench seat that shrinks in increments
      mile by mile.

Leather-seamed real estate lines
imagined centrifugal force
and the unscientific but powerful
counter-centrifugal force
has us flinging our bodies
back and forth into each other until
the Gran Torino

plunges through the bright tunnel
beneath the Hudson River.
We are
vacuum-packed in awe,
emerging to greet
the Manhattan skyline
blinking and winking
holding the unspoken wild promise of
everything.

The wind is knocked out of
our petty sibling clashes
as we float over the Brooklyn Bridge
breathless because
there she is,
standing tall and unmoving
like an illuminated hallucination
saying all are welcome
to New York.

Runner-Up

Mom should've been a model
everyone says.

Wide eyes
with green-colored contacts,
cheekbones tuned to max volume
heart-shaped face framed
with flirty
summer-blond hair.
"If anyone asks, I'm a
natural blonde," she tells me,
as her mother told her,
"That's exactly
what it says
on the bottle after all."
Mom reaffirms it each month
with a box from the drugstore.

She is thin-thin-thin
and everything
else that a woman should be.
Enchanting my father so absolutely.
He calls her Lady Godiva
with nude desire uncomfortable to witness.
Like they're alone
with their lust.

My mother turns heads
on the street
at the mall
even in church.

The neighbors wait, as she
gets ready, pulls on shorts
laces up sneakers, clips on Walkman, then
base / concealer / eyeliner / lipstick / powder / mascara /
and blush that is wasted on a
face soon flushed
as she jogs along the road.
Tears of sweat,
milky with foundation,
flow down her neck as she
            parades   past.

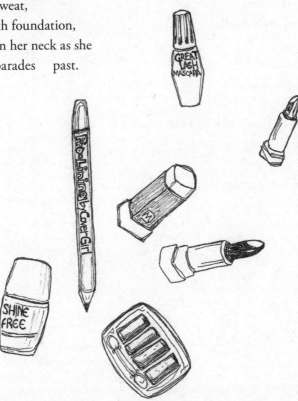

Health Food Bites

Mom embraces
the natural food movement
and is an instant zealot.
HEALTH FOOD is our new way of life.
In place of chocolate? Carob—
        and carob is revolting.
Raisins for dessert—
        but raisins are *not* dessert!
Have Mom's taste buds
dribbled out of her mouth
as she smiles
blissfully feeding us
corrugated cardboard?

Health potions
the manifestation of love.
The foul flavor *flavor* **flavor**
of fishy-tasting capsules and oils
repeating all *urp* day long.

I teach myself to palm
Dad's Chips Ahoy!s
as I stroll casually by.

Wild Horses

A girl in my class
is effortlessly
unquestioningly worshipped and
loves horses so much
everyone
in her gravitational field
       loves horses now.
She brings
painted horse models
to school
bestows them
one by one
upon the worthy.
A growing herd
of prancing beauties
day by day,
more and more
enthusiastically corralled
across smooth desktops.
The luckiest earn
coveted blond equines
preening and posing
manes flowing
in invisible wind.

And my desk is an empty acre.

Burning shame
colors my days.

Excluded from the game
of being included.

Saturday afternoon
my family walks through
the big red doors
of Arnold's Toy Store,
my heart lunges at
one lonely, untamed horse, tan and dusty
galloping under glass.
I point, eager, eager—
but the ask is caught in my throat.

We're all being careful today.

One wrong step will detonate
Mom's land-mine fury at Dad
for disappearing
into drinking last night.
This family stroll down Main Street
his weary bloodshot penance.
Dad points out
train sets
rainbow puzzles
magic kits
and waves stuffed animals
in Christopher's and Cara's faces
till they giggle,
unwinding the spring trigger
on Mom's rage.

Who cares about
plain pretty horses anyway? I
always liked unicorns.

Plan BC3

Mom enrolls Dad in night class
at Butler County Community College
a mile down our winding road.
He just needs a higher education
       and to maybe stop
       getting high with the paperboy
to become a better man.
But old high school habits die hard.
Each week Dad skips
growing chunks of class time,
sneaking cigarettes in the bathroom
until finally
he's going out drinking
instead of showing up for class at all.

Mom is furious
when he flunks,
but Dad is a salesman who can sell
anything, especially to her.
She was obviously wrong
to push him.

Hear Her Roar

Mom enrolls *herself* in night class
at Butler County Community College
a mile down our winding road.
My grandfather cries
    really cries
thinks more bright and shining dreams
will only break her heart more.

She raises the stakes,
transfers to
Slippery Rock University,
a whole half hour away.
Exhilarated. Grabbing
college credit by college credit
like spread-out
crumbs on a trail,
she trudges toward
a psychology degree
that "nobody can ever take away."

Our perfect Mom
gets perfect grades,
highlighting textbooks
with taxi-yellow markers,
reading all her class notes
into a recorder that
repeats over
and over
and over
until we all recite

psychological disorders
in our sleep.

No time for baking bread
singing songs in the kitchen
drawing, sewing
reading just for fun
as Mom collects **A**s
like **Good Job** smiley stickers,
and laughs
when her younger classmates
complain she's wrecking the curve.

I tuck "the kids" into bed
round heads that don't lay still
round eyes that pop wide
with any hint of the Best Big Sister Ever
trying to escape in the dark.
Mom sits alone
at our round kitchen table
into the yawning night.
Slim fingers dancing
on the yard sale typewriter
     Click-Click-Click *ding*
     Click-Click-Click *ding*
tap-tap-tapping away
at her new dream.

Movin' On Up

Wooden plaques
proudly line the mantle.
Sales awards that stack up to a
big promotion with
a brand-new blue
Chevy Celebrity
company car.

Engraved awards
next to dented cooking pots that ping
with each drip of water they catch
from our stained brown ceiling.

Dad's promotion prompts
Mom to hunt down
the perfect plot of property
where we can build a brand-new house.

The day they pour the foundation
we pile into the Celebrity
rushing with excitement to see.

I find a loose nail
and drag it through the cement
writing all our names,
even the cats.
Claiming that basement-to-be as *ours*.
The smooth gray slab seems small.
Our house will be humble but
fresh and
so brand-new.

Mom pores over carpet swatches,
countertop samples, and
blueprints.
Adding more windows,
        more windows, more windows.
Planning for all that fresh natural light
to shine beautiful and bright
into our brand-new start.

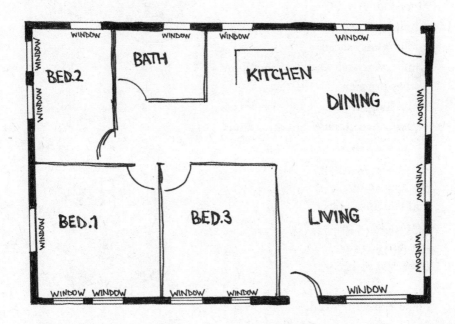

The New Girl

At my new school
some kids barely notice
there's a new girl in the sixth grade.
Some kids dub me "Miss Perfect,"
act as if I think I'm better than them
which is dumb because I don't.

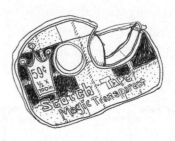

Some kids
admire the new girl's pin-straight hair
and its glossy sheen.
I smile wide and revel in their approval
as they privately
weave long strips
of sticky Scotch tape into my strands.

Some kids are quiet
shy and weird
and safe, misfits who
don't poke or prod
but instead orbit
in benign silence.

Some kids write words
in the margins of the chalkboard
when the teacher isn't looking.
Ugly words, about
how the new girl has buck teeth
from sucking dicks.

But it's not like I can take
anything personally.
Nobody here
even knows me.
And that sucking dicks thing?
So far outside
the realm of reality,
it's almost funny
almost.

Granny

In New York
we stay at Mom's
growing-up house in Queens,
my ~~hitman~~ grandfather now
kicked out for having a mistress,
where Mom's mom has stopped
taking bullshit from anybody.

Mom's mom is "Granny,"
but ironically,
she never cooks or bakes or sews,
dresses chic
works in publishing
smokes with graceful flourish
forever trying
to lose ten pounds.

She and Mom
in the kitchen discuss
how they long to shed their

big, wide butts
The Family Curse

while playing hairdresser
with boxes
of wavy, blond beauty.

I beg Granny until she agrees
to give my straight, stringy hair
a home permanent
to match Mom's.
The rotten egg smell
chases cigarette smoke
from the small
yellow kitchen.
Granny wraps sections of hair
in paper squares,
rolls it
tighter than I imagined
on thin pink plastic rods,
stops to draw from
a lipstick-covered butt,
and warns
"perms are unpredictable."

Predictably
     frizz frizz frizz
my perm looks nothing like Mom's soft curls.
I'm miles from
the glamorous girl on the box
and realize that family curse
is hitting me hard
right where I sit.

Sky Jumper

The first time I climbed to the top
of the way high dive
I was seven and afraid to jump,
wanted to retreat back down that
long
long
long
long
ladder.

I stood shaking, hugging myself,
caught between glory and shame.

And then I saw my dad
treading calmly in the water below.
"It's okay," he called, "I've got you."
And there was no courage in me,
only trust in him,
as I stepped into space and flew.

Hide and Leak

For someone trying
to conceal evidence
he's been drinking
Dad's pretty lousy
at concealing evidence
he's been drinking.

Tucked inside
a basket of laundry
I find a glass bottle
red cap
half-filled with clear booze.
My breath pulls in.
I don't want to touch it,
use dirty clothes to
shove it down, down
under socks and wrinkled T-shirts.
Hide his secret better for him.

On the floor of the Celebrity's back seat
I discover a fat wine bottle
empty on its side.
I falter,
kick it deep under the front seat,
concealing his carelessness.

When I hear Mom's yells
floating from the garage
and Dad's claim he
      loaned the car to a friend
      doesn't even like wine
      she's acting crazy,

I swallow the bile of my guilt,
silently will Mom to
doubt herself
believe him.

She comes upstairs
cheeks flushed, eyes blazing
snaps at my staring,
"Nothing's wrong. Go to your room."

Clinging to a shrinking raft of denial,
I feel helpless
acquire a habit
smelling Dad for alcohol
automatically, anytime he's near.
Especially if he's happy.
Human Breathalyzer,
        now there's a skill
everything hinging
on that
sweet, smothering scent
that sinks my hope.
        Dad's drinking again.

Fast Times, circa 1983

I'm too
mature, too
advanced, far too
old to watch Cara and Christopher's
Saturday morning cartoons
Smurfs and Care Bears and He-Man.

Even Scooby-Scooby-*Scooby-Doo!*
feels so repetitive and childish.

But Christopher
lines couch cushions along our floor,
Cara piles up blankets galore,
sprinkles pillows on top the rest
making such a snug, inviting nest,
I can't seem to disengage and
. . . if it wasn't for you meddling kids . . .
I kick off my shoes
and don't act my age.

Besties Fer Sure

My closest friend
goes to my church where we
"youths" meet every Wednesday night
to play icebreakers
practice flirting
and pray.
Samantha is cute and petite,
the Shirley Feeney to my
gangly, poor-postured Laverne.

We spend hours
tethered
by curlicued phone cords
that conduct
gossip about what the *bad kids* are doing.
Marveling
that people our age
drink and smoke pot and presumably
don't care about brain cells functioning.
And sex!
Risk pregnancy?
Why tempt wreckage like that?
How do they not care what anyone thinks?
What *everyone* thinks.

We theorize bra stuffing
by a showy, singing girl,
skinny everywhere but her boobs.
Our rumor busted by a youth trip
to the water park.
Worse, all must wait as
red-faced, I wrestle jeans vs. damp legs.

I bring my boom box to Samantha's
for sleepovers.
We choreograph dance moves to
mixtapes featuring
Madonna and Michael and Cyndi,
practice Valley Girl impressions,
whispering the word *bitchin'*
laughing at ourselves
until our stomach muscles ache.
Fully aware
of what huge nerds we each are.
But together, we're,
like, *totally fer sure* awesome.

Hear Me

I cannot help that
my volume dial is broken
I am loud
too loud
and excitable
and when I'm excited?
Way too LOUD.
Forget myself until I hear "shhhhh,"
like ice water tossed in my face.
Reminding me I'm too much.
Should be less.

I hate the absoluteness of me.

Try to act laid back
but forget myself
constantly exposed by
a suicide vest of
laughter bursting from my chest
drawing stares,
reminding me I need to be cool
stop being
too much
too big
too earnest
too intense-in-your-face
too   freaking   loud.

Ch-Ch-Ch-Changes

Everything I've known is ending
like a really good book I don't want to finish
because I will miss being in that world.
      Everything is changing . . .

Mom's earned her straight A master's,
now a high school special education teacher,
putting me in charge after school.
      Everything is changing . . .

including at church,
a new pastor who *rants*
about the 7-Eleven
with its video games and magazines.
No word of hope for those who,
as Mom says, "managed to drag
our sin-bloated bodies" to a pew.
No lightness. No victory.
No point waking up early
every Sunday.
      Everything is changing . . .

including my body too much, too fast.
Circus tall with Popeye calves
and saddlebags, a "friend" points out.
      Everything is changing . . .

A boy hisses, "eat me,"
in the back of the art room,
gesturing to his acid wash crotch.
He repeats his suggestion
until my cheeks go hot, and I
back away to my seat.
He and I used to laugh together,
sniffing scented magic markers
instead of coloring our
maps of the world,
suggesting, "Smell this,"
only to hit each other's hands,
        forcing marker tip to nose
teacher scolding our squeals of delight,
and matching rainbow freckles,
but there's no teacher here,
and I'm afraid of him now,
        and everything is changing.

Ch-Ch-Ch-Changes, Part 2

Everything changing is
not exactly *horrible,*
if I'm *completely* honest,
fifteen is
on occasion
exhilarating
my insides
waking the hell up
to how one quick look
from the right boy
flash floods my lower belly
which swirls and shouts
sometimes change is
good.

Tongue-Tied

Talking to boys
be hard for me
with clever the words
coming only
after they've gone.

Lucy

I like the way
Mom and Dad
fight calm and cool
through clenched teeth at Granny's,
not hot and loud
like at home.
I love the sport of
chasing down
the ice-cream truck
anytime its upbeat jingle hits our ears.
There is no Mister Softee in PA,
definitely no
cute older neighbor boys
like the ones playing
street hockey on Granny's block.

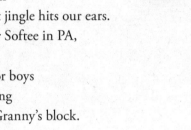

But my favorite part
of New York
is my cousin.

Lucy, four years older and
massively cooler.
Our lives
so far apart, yet
this must be what
having the best big sister ever is like. And I *love* it.

Bitingly funny,
she can tell a story so well
it makes you wish
you were there for the adventure,
even if you were.

Lucy is always banker for Monopoly,
inventing random loophole rules
that play to her favor,
but she's generous with
her coveted collection
of *Mad* magazines.

She makes up contests
to see who can eat
the most at breakfast.
She's stuffing slices of toast
while I spoon bowls of Freakies with milk.

I copy her thick black eyeliner
beg to get my ears pierced
to wear feather earrings like her.
Faithfully mimic
her strong hand gestures and
heavy New Yawk accent.

She is fun fun fun
with short blond hair that flips
and a smile that catches.
Maybe she'd see how pretty
if my mom wasn't
wrecking the curve.

Lucy is unhappy with her body,
      the family curse
      at her back
drinks Tab
by the liter.
Her size fluctuates between visits,
but her self-loathing
stays the same.

Perchance to Dream

I am fifteen and a half
Lucy nineteen
the Christmas we lounge
on the stiff plaid couches
eating Breyer's
coffee ice cream from the carton
immersed in the blue radiance
of a *Twilight Zone* rerun.

We assault our fat in stereo
prompting a pact.

Chucking our spoons
in the sink,
we weigh in
on the compliant bathroom scale.
A new contest.
No inventing random rules.
Whoever loses weight
the fastest
wins.
No loopholes this time.

The Glossies

Glamour
Vogue
Elle
Bazaar
even *Seventeen,*
"Where the Girl Ends
and the Woman Begins."
I buy them all.
Their polished pages
exhausted
within days
and I'm waiting
for *Next Month!*'s issue.
I barely notice
the cutting-edge fashion; I'm
too busy studying the models,
looking at
smooth skin
pursed lips
sightless staring
taunting me
chanting mutely,
Join us.
Be beautiful.
Become immortal.
Thin alone may enter.

I mimic their poses
but hope drains away.

You'll never be one of them.
Your body's all wrong.

Ass Inspector

I compare my ~~butt~~

                    family curse

to all the girls

        at school

                in the mall

       along the street,

on TV.

I can't help

but look for reassurance

that my bottom end is okay,

that I'm not uniquely deformed.

          Comfort never comes.

People likely wonder

why I'm constantly checking out

other girl's butts.

Calvin Klein Jeans

Imposter

7:50 AM., Knoch High School, Saxonburg, PA

brrrring

The bell
launches the adolescent fashion show,
up and down the hallways.
Big, crispy Aqua Net hair
thick eyebrows
Day-Glo
     everywhere.

     Vibrant comb handles spring
     from back pockets of
     tight! designer! jeans!
     Bonjour, Gloria Vanderbilt, Guess, and
        for the girls with
   the luckiest butts: Oooh-la-la Sasson
embroidered hind ends
mocking me in my basic bargain Lees.

Finally, a blowout sale
on Jordache jeans
means Mom indulges me
a painfully tight pair

        must compress
       that humiliating ass of yours.
The ad plays in my head as I
struggle to close the sturdy brass fly.
She's got the look! *pant pant suck*
She's got the look! *ungh*
ziiip *That Jordache Look!*

My stomach looks flat,
but so does my butt,
and no matter how much mousse I use,
my hair's flat too.
Feather earrings don't vibe
with cheap knockoff polos
whose collars won't stay popped.
Casually, I pull on knit leg warmers,
slide a braided purple headband
under perky side pony, but
I'm honestly trying here.
I care way too much, and I
don't know what the hell I'm doing.

Emergency Drill

The alarm blares
announcing our schoolwide tornado drill.
Obedient hostages, we shuffle out of classrooms
line up against both sides of the hall
turn to face the wall and sit down.
ungh My Jordache Look slices
deep into my stomach. *pant pant*

We are to
place our hands on the backs of our heads
lean foreheads against the wall.
But I can barely make my jean-bound legs
criss-cross applesauce.
No way can I fold in half.

"Be sure to open your mouths wide
to balance the pressure in your ears,"
the teachers say.
We laugh because
everybody knows.
Ears pop, pop, popping
would be the least of our worries
if this mythical twister
ripped through our school.

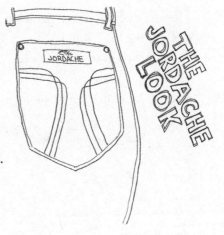

This torturous practicing is pointless.
What can we do
to prevent tornado season
but pray we aren't all
blown away?

Imposter 2

Dark denim slides along green pleather
near the back of the bus, my daydream
interrupted by,
"How many pairs
of Jordache do you own?"

Carol,
> the chalkboard poet
> who so cleverly coupled
> buck teeth and blow jobs,

sits behind me every day
the half-hour ride
to and from school.

My tongue slides
across metal braces,
"These are my only pair."

The way she whispers to her seatmate
reminds me,
I'm on my third wear this week.
Can't help but love
their leg-numbing denim goodness,

Dang. Should've lied.

Imposter 3

At the mall, I ask my parents
for the *right* brand. White leather
chubby rubber soles.
Stan Smith is the man! *Whoever he is.*
Mom and Dad kindly indulge me
with strained looks on eager faces.
The bored clerk in a referee shirt
laces me up indifferently as my heart pounds
with the guilt of my greed,
and the way
the expensive shoes look all wrong
on my enormous feet.

Found Mainstream Media

Losing weight is delicious! Now you can look
better than ever. Take off the weight you hate!
Beat the battle of the bulge!
Now you see it . . . now you don't!
Start losing today!

How to have a sensational body!
How to look fit, firm, and terrific.
How to get a long lean body.

YOUR BODY:
shape it up,
slim it down,
polish it up for summer.
Lose weight just in time for summer!
Hot Stuff! 100 slimming summer looks!

You! Slim and Trim! SO SLEEK! Secrets
of staying THIN. Slim down now!

Solve your biggest body problems.
Longer, leaner legs!
Fast trimmers for upper body flab.
Flatten your belly. Fast track
to a lean sexy belly. How'd she get those
abs? Your best abs ever!
Flat abs fast

Flat abs NOW

Flat abs. Sculpted arms. Tight butt.
Flat abs!
Firm butt!
Lean thighs!
No more jiggle! Lose your belly. Get a cute butt!

FOOD TRAPS: eating at the movies,
the ball game,
the mall.
                    Fabulous body firm-up.
                    Easy slim-down diet!
Sensational fruit diet
The Eat Out Diet
The supermodel diet!
Dancing diet!
                It could work for you too!
Super diet! Twenty best diet tips.
            Lose 15 pounds in one month!
                        Shed fat   fast!
THIN-AT-
                    LAST!
How to lose those
                last
stubborn ten pounds! 10 tricks
to tame your appetite.

Fat to fabulous in only seven days!
Peel off seven pounds in seven days!
    Seven-day detox. Sleek in a week!
    6 steps to a great body!
    Six workouts for a sexy shape.
                    Melt away
                5 pounds in 5 days!
            Get Flat Abs in 4 Fun Steps.
BLITZ DIET! 3 pounds in 3 days!
Shed one size!
Shed two sizes!
Lose all the weight you want.

Results not typical

No Can Do

Overwhelmed by choices,
feats and fears, careers to conquer.
A list of professions jeers from a bulletin board, mocking,
doctorteacherlawyeraccountanttherapist.
The possibilities infinite and
       ohsoverypressing.
"What are your interests?" the guidance counselor asks
too brightly,
"People are usually good at doing things they like,
and they usually like doing things they're good at. Heh."

My only As are in creative writing.
I crave teacher's ~~love~~ responses to my work.
Can't hide my grin reading their notes
       Mr. Mortimer says I have ***talent*** but warns
writing is not an easy life,
and based on my all-late assignments,
I lack the discipline of deadlines.

Charcoals and mâché
are not a career
unless I want to teach crafts
       to children? *Ew.*
I'm steered into structural design.
The tests say ☑I ☑can ☑be ☑an ☑architect.

A two-hour pilgrimage on a field-trip bus,
I fall for Fallingwater.
The iconic house and woods are one,
the design pure art, but
my blueprints are more M. C. Escher than Frank Lloyd Wright.
My visions ⁓mapped dream objects⁓
turns out, architecting uses so much math.

I decide:
No matter what I accomplish
who I become
1) I must be thin or 2) nothing 3) else 4) counts.

Thin is better
does not need proving.
Just look around
all desperate to lose weight.

Those lucky enough to be thin are just that ★Lucky★

As for the rest of us? We

are   *Tragic*

Maybe I'll just start there

and

hope

the

rest

falls

into

place.

The Diet

It has finally come in the mail.
The "Cost Good Money" diet that Mom ordered, for me.
She's so excited. To bond.
My very first weight-loss plan.
          Where *is* that baby book?

Side by side, we spread
colorful laminated cards across my bed.
Stacks of blue and green and orange.
Meals doled out like hall passes
granting permission to eat.

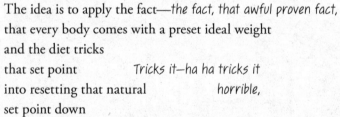

We study instructions,
          reading together like
          before Cara and Christopher.
The idea is to apply the fact—*the fact, that awful proven fact,*
that every body comes with a preset ideal weight
and the diet tricks
that set point   *Tricks it—ha ha tricks it*
into resetting that natural   *horrible,*
set point down

                  down

                  down.

It makes perfect sense really
metabolism and genetics and science
          all explained in the literature.
"Eeeeeeeeeeee!"
                  You're going to be thin!

What a great feeling.
Mom and I hug.

The plan seems tolerable
but it soon grows apparent
between my not-a-morning-person breakfasts
school-bought lunches and
working-mother dinners
I really can't make my eating fit their rules,

so despite
all that good money spent, my

                horrible
                hideous
                repulsive

natural set point
Stays Put.

Gospel Truth

I sit on my

                     ample

ass at church
with my small breasts

         and thick legs.
       Just look at the way
     your thighs fuse together
     and ooze across the pew.

Through a haze of dark thoughts
I hear Ephesians 5:29:
"After all,
no one ever hated their own body . . ."

and I want to stand on my seat
point and shout,

"Bullshit!"

Sequinettes

I try out for the kickline squad
don't make it,
despite the fact that
they're so hard up for members
they have
a second round of tryouts.
So I shamelessly try out again.

Samantha is over
when I get the call
from the captain sharing the
super! great! news!
that *this time* I've made the squad.

I leap up and down
squeal with excitement
this changes everything.

It changes who I am.

The Breakfast Club recently opened my eyes.
I'm ready to be a Ringwaldian princess
        cue my makeover montage.

Samantha doesn't understand,
        trying to bring me down,
        leaving early because
~~I'm being obnoxious~~ she's jealous.

For days I wear the
super! great! news!
on my face
a perpetual grin.
Two upperclassmen
tip heads together,
discuss the new drill team lineup
in loud whispers. Say,
"How *sad*
the captains needed two tryouts
because the new recruits are all
so *pathetic*. Guess who even
made the cut . . ."

They turn,
look at me,
look at each other
      and laugh.
Face burning, I smooth
my shirt over
          that humiliating rim of pudge
              exploding above
the waistband of my jeans.

Sticking Keds
over my big feet,
pulling a short dance team skirt
over my ample ass, and
punching pom-poms in the air
at five, six, seven, eight . . .
has zero effect on
my popularity.

Just makes my Popeye calves
bigger from all the marching.
And nobody gives   a   shit
where   I   fit
but me.

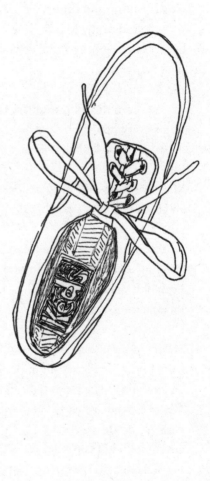
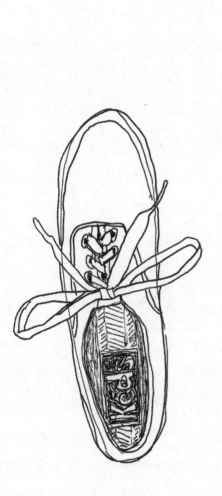

First Kiss

I thank God for sending Jonathan
to youth group
just for me.
Good-looking and funny
            and funny-looking and good,
he loves boring beige computers even more
than Samantha,
can solve any Rubik's Cube
            even the mini-necklace one I wear.

Beeps every hour from his
digital Casio calculator watch.
Like a sexy
Matthew Broderick in *WarGames*
and he is one of the rare boys
taller than me.

Based on the way acidic juices
flood my body when he's around,
I can only assume
Jonathan is exactly my type.

He draws me clever comics, and I
write him funny letters in pink ink
on loose-leaf folded into tight footballs.
We hold hands when
parents and the pastor
aren't looking. I can't control
my blushing, and we are almost immediately
an official "going together" couple.

After an acoustic guitar praise circle
in our youth leader's backyard,
we sneak into the autumn woods.

Walking hand in hand, both knowing
we're on a mission to kiss.
      An event we have
      negotiated *at length*
      via human telephone
          through his best friend
          and Samantha.

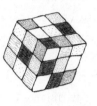

Dry leaves crunch under our feet,
the scent of the pines surrounds us like incense,
as sweat **delicately drips**
from my pits.

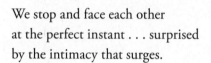

We stop and face each other
at the perfect instant . . . surprised
by the intimacy that surges.

My every cell is conscious of
the closeness of our bodies,
soft lips fall open, and I
know him better, more fully
connected on a deeper
plane that suddenly exists.
Nothing else matters.
I allow myself to fall fully,
and it tastes **solid** and **pure** and **free** . . .

except my elbows
glued down to hide sweaty pits,
the sharp scrape of metal, as braces bump,
and holding my breath
so I don't puff warm nose air
onto Jonathan's cheek.

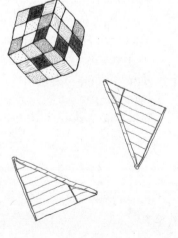

Trapper Keeper Treason

A cute, popular boy sits
behind me in history.
A football player who
makes history Suck Less.

Our flirting is
            harmless.
He is so far
            from my league,
we play different sports
            plus
I have all the wrong equipment.

Besides,
Jonathan is the love of my life.

Until that cute popular boy runs the toe
of his rubber-soled Nikes
slowly down the inner-arch of my Stan Smiths
and sends such aching through me . . .

I grab my Trapper Keeper,
to start crossing out
doodled rows of Jonathans
before he can see
how all the *o*'s are little hearts.

Break Up

Next youth group
is completely different.
Jonathan's small inside jokes
about marshmallows and "moo juice"
that normally get me giggling,
are pushpins in my chest,
          puncturing our best Polaroids.
Instead, awkwardness
hangs heavy
in the air,
signaling *something's wrong,*
so he won't be shocked when
"we have to talk"
at the end of the night.

His expression is grim
as I lead him to our private spot
between the church's two brick buildings.
Our make-out space
that I am here to vandalize.

I tried writing a note.
But the warmth and humor
that leaked from my pen,
made it seem like a joke.

It feels like one.
Why am I breaking up
with my own heart?

Blinking, I see myself
on the beefy arm
of the cute popular boy.
And know I need
to release Jonathan.
Cannot cheat on him,
not for one second
not even in my mind.

I stand, facing him.
No game of telephone.
No folded-up note.
Only crossed arms
and anguished expression.
Everything in me
wants to slow time down . . .
wait . . .
I'm not sure . . .

I force the words "this isn't working"
through my lips, each syllable
a lie.
This has been working fine.
One week ago, he was the best part of my life.

Like a prophet, he asks if I like someone else.
I hate how dirty it feels
to nod *yes*.
I wasn't trying to.

Jonathan is *so understanding.*
We share a miserable hug,
fight off tears, and my mind

flip-flops frantically. I wish I'd known
our last kiss would be the last. Want
"please one more?"

But his expression
turns him into someone else
who looks at me
like I can't be trusted.
He says it's
"not a good idea," and I
pretend
to agree.

Aftermath

The moment I step into my bedroom,
I'm attacked by grief
waiting for me in the dark.
It jumps on my back,
flings me violently across my bed,
presses my face into my pillow,
and pulls out all my stuffing like a dog.

I didn't realize how much I loved
knowing Jonathan was mine.
I want to take back the breakup. How could I be
so stupid and impulsive? I've ruined
everything. And it takes far too many days
of sitting in history class with my toes stretched
way, way back to realize
that footsie moment of clarity
must have been a misunderstanding. Or maybe a
Bloopers & Practical Jokes-style prank.
Love is not waiting for me
around every corner
the way Jonathan made it seem it would be.

He set me up to trust and have faith,
to see myself as deserving of love,
and that was his one
true cruelty.

Drowning

Mom and Dad fight at night
smashing fragile family joy
      with words.
I am full of dread,
afraid that Cara and Christopher
      the kids
will wake and hear.
The grown-ups now the ones making
      all that racket.
I am
helpless. Can't stop
anything,
including the tears on my pillow
that pool into sleep.
I dream that my bed is being pitched about by a sea of black
flowing roughly through my room.
Blacker than the color black
the empty black
      of void.

I cling to the familiar white headboard of my raft until
everything is falling . . .

falling . . .

I flinch awake,
pulled back into
my parents' screams of hate.

Sweet Sixteen

Legend has it
sixteen years ago today,
I was a compact infant
swaddled in pale pink.
The nurse strode in on her thick white nurse shoes,
held me up in the air,
and reported happily to my parents,
"We're calling this one the *Guzzler*."

Drowning 2

Mom and Dad fight ~~at night~~,
smashing ~~fragile family joy~~
with words.
I am ~~full of dread,~~
afraid that Cara and Christopher
   the kids
will ~~wake and~~ hear.

Everything is ~~falling . . .~~

falling . . .

I ~~flinch~~ awake,
~~plunged back~~ into
my parents' screams of hate.

Pod People

From the outside, *we look good.*
The five of us file out the door
our church shoes *click-click-clicking.*
If we can only
make it to our pew
sit up straight, hair combed
teeth brushed,
Dad's wide tie even
Mom's makeup in place, then *everything*
will be okay.

My friends tell me that I have
       such a *handsome* father
            a *beautiful* mother
                  adorable sister and brother.
            What the heck happened to you? Ha ha.
They are all so envious with their own
frumpy, old, plain-looking parents.

We look good,
but I know we are
holding our fingers in cracks as we smile.
Hey, we're happy.
Doing just fine, thanks.
No problems
here.

Drowning 3

Mom and Dad fight at night,
smashing fragile family joy

█████████

I am █████████

afraid ████████████

█████████

█████████

Everything is ███████

███████

███████

plunged ██ in ██

██████████ hate.

Game of Chicken

Dad is heading out to play ball with his buddies.
Mom suggests he take the kids and me along.
His word he won't drink tonight
not enough, voices rise
tempers flare, and finally,
he puts on a smirk and asks us,
"Ready to watch your dad play some ball?"
like this was his idea all along.

When we get to the field
he tells us to go ahead,
he'll meet us at the dugout.
I hold two small hands
turn back and catch him
standing by the trunk,
bottle to lips.
I'm glad Mom's not here. He is
Pinocchio in silhouette.

I forgot to bring a book,
so I play in the dirt with Cara and Chris until
streaks of dust darken our arms and legs.

Hours later, Dad yells overly loud goodbyes
out the open window
while steering us out of the lot.
I wonder if he remembered
the blasphemous bottle *(bottles?)* from the trunk.

And
then

we are speeding and passing a car on the wrong side of the road,
which is totally fine with this type of long, straight stretch of road
with dotted yellow lines. Everything's okay, except that this is not
okay at all because right now there is a car coming toward us closer
and closer and closer so fast that I realize that Dad is more drunk
and less Dad, and I pull my dirt-streaked legs to my chest and turn
into a ball on the passenger seat, shut my eyes, and pray *please, Jesus,*
and the long honk of the oncoming car slides by us so close it marks
my shift

to Mom's side.

Stuck in the Sky

I'm back
on that way high dive,
disoriented,
too high up that
long
long
long
long
ladder.
What made me think
I could fly?

I am helpless,
and exposed.

And Dad is *not*
treading calmly in the water below.
Even if he was, how could he help?
Wouldn't we both just drown in the deep?
I can't believe I was so impulsive
so trusting.
I'm holding up the line.

     Move it, pigbitch.

I never want to feel
this out of control again.

MADD

It is late and we're all in bed—that is,
except for Dad who didn't come home. Again.
But there is something different,
an electric current of shared intuition
running through Mom and me,
sparking us to spring when the phone rings, like
something's wrong.

We stand in nightshirts as Mom answers.

Dad's friend says Dad left drunk, and he's sorry
he couldn't convince him not to, but Mom says
it's not his fault, Dad's a grown man, and she and I hit
snooze on our dread and go back to bed.

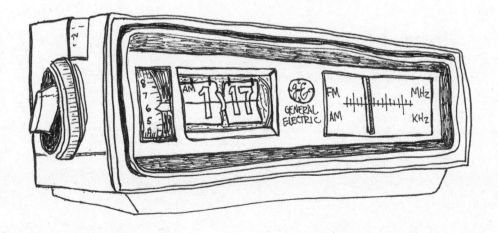

Broken Snooze Button

In the morning
Mom is years older.
She intercepts me before
I reach her bedroom.

I ask if Daddy's home, and her "yes" is a relief—but
there was an accident, he looks pretty bad, and
may get sent to jail. Dad may go to jail.

Gravely, I nod, call to him through the bedroom door. His voice
drips with sympathy for me having to see him like
this as I step into the room.

He is so sorry.

Black floss, like
Mom and I used when we sewed
cross-stitch, zigs and zags

across purple-and-yellow eyebrow.
Frankenstein, says a voice in my
head. The air in the room

swells so thick, is too dense to
breathe. Dad's pleading voice breaks,
and Mom shoos me away from

my handsome dad,
my handsome dad,
my handsome dad.

Junk Yard Dog

I go with Dad to get
stuff out of the car
he wrecked.
The new company car because
the old company fired him for drinking
on the job, and so now he will need to
find another company and clearly
another car.

The windshield has a crackled tumor
the exact same shape
as his head, dried blood drips
down the steering wheel

a beer can watches from the floor,
mouth dropped open
in hollow surprise, how does

safety glass
work anyway,

the windshield shattered yet
holding itself together in
the perfect mold of Daddy's head?

Shrine

My wooden box of art supplies
gathers dust under my bed alongside
a collection of dirty dishes, and colonies
of unwashed underwear and socks.
Left-over-cereal-milk
thickens to yogurt surprisingly quick.
Mom says I'm a slob, but
it's just that artistic temperament from
when I imagined I was a real artist.

Until fresh inspiration strikes
for a makeup station
inside my closet.
I run an extension cord for a light-up mirror
salvage a child-sized chair from the garage.
My studio complete,
I tuck myself behind
the curtain of clothes,
spend hours worshipping
at my aptly named vanity.
Desperate.

I sit. I stare.
I stare. I sit.

Brown eyes blink back underneath
brown bangs I cut too short. Again.
The crunch of scissors
cutting hair so satisfying,
the results repeatedly
unsettling.

                    Unfortunate habit,
             that face is basic and boring,
wide forehead, scoop nose,
nice cheekbones—thanks Mom.
Smile is decent now the braces are off,
                    buckteeth half-tamed.

But
                    nope, not beautiful

my one possible path to
beautiful
is artfully applied cosmetics
             Can't you at least draw attention
                    from that fleshy double chin?
I collect a mass of dollar makeup
from the drugstore clearance bin,
sprinkle in Mom's rejected colors,
organize everything
into my pink Caboodle.
My new art kit.

The Joy of Painting

Slather on a beige base coat
        create a smooth, clear canvas.
Carefully, select an eye shadow palette
        color choice is up to me.
Brush on mascara, contour with blush
        making happy little cheeks!
Pale, shimmering pink for
        happy little lips!
Bob Ross is right—
        anyone can do this.

Two / Girl Unglued

Whistleblower

Mom invites me to take a walk
in the woods by our house,
talks to me like I'm an adult now.

She'll be needing more help with the kids.
Dad's not going to jail after all. He's going to rehab.
"Sometimes people can't help what they are. Your dad
is an alcoholic."

She explains
our need to understand
and forgive.
Dad has a disease.
We walk side by side.
Mud clings to the soles of our boots.
Light bobs through the branches of the trees
like I'm underwater.

I tell Mom she can count on me,
and when we step out of the woods,
we're a team.

A Few Parting Gifts

Mom dropped Cara, Chris, and I
at the mall to pick
a present to give Dad
for his rehab trip.
Where he can get better,
where there are people who can
                                                    help.

We are serious about our assignment, searching
for the perfect item that will remind
Dad to really try for us,
for less than eight dollars.

Nine-year-old Chris is excited when he spots
the "Look, look, look, perfect gift!"
A bottle opener–key chain
with the Budweiser logo inscribed.
"Dad loves Budweiser."

Ten-year-old Cara and I
look at each other.

The uncomfortable silence
makes way for grins
that grow into snickers,
giving birth to giggles and then
full-blown *laughter*.
Chris gives a small, shy smile,
says *"Oh,"*
and it feels
like things might be okay as we
walk through the mall alone together.

Batteries Not Included

Apparently, rehabs don't always "take."
Dad ends up getting drunk again, and
Mom has him put in the hospital
to detox.

He runs away, and I hear him
screaming at her
how awful it was
how evil she is
for forcing him there.

"There was a girl there whose eyes were
black." He repeats again and again,
"Black, doyouhearme, completely black!"

And I want to ask him
about that girl. Want to know
how she got that way,
if one can see with blackened eyes but
cannot mention anything about the fight

because that would acknowledge the fight, and
in this beautiful family
n o b o d y   f i g h t s.

A Knight's Tail

Alice is a delicate tabby
we adopted.
Arthur is a big gray tomcat who adopted us.
Cara and Chris
dress them in doll clothes,
conduct weekly wedding ceremonies
while yellow eyes glare.
Escaping zealous affection,
Alice and Arthur honeymoon together
at that exquisite windowfront getaway
where the sun beams in strong.
The two of them
fold together and bake.

Two uninvited Irish setters
gallop their purebred selves
into our mixed-breed yard,
run wild circles
celebrating their luck of
a gate left open.
We laugh
until they chase our cats,
then yell for them to "GET!"
Arthur protects his Alice,
defending her honor
with bold hisses and spits
gray tail puffed as he
bluffs with small, sharp claws exposed.
The dogs are delighted by his challenge,
and Arthur is playfully
caught up like a ragdoll.

Mom throws lawn furniture.
I shout and give chase as Chris
runs inside to wake Dad
from his longstanding couch nap.
I punch-punch-punch
one big red dog
as he shake-shake-shakes
our brave cat
Arthur goes limp
and flop-flop-flops
to the ground.

Dad rouses from the hollers
to see Chris standing rigid,
caught-caught-caught
between being a boy wary
of his mystical father
and being the only
man of the house who is conscious.

By the time Dad runs out,
hair sticking up, he's
too late to do anything
except bury valiant Arthur in our field.

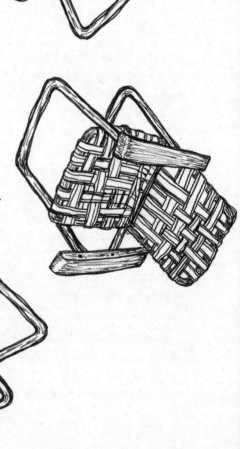

King's Ransom

Dad brings me with him
down the road to confront
the big red dogs' careless owners.
He clangs the brass knocker
on their glossy, varnished door.
When they answer, Dad yells while I
cry, and the people are
so sorry about our cat.

They promise
to keep their dogs tied up,
offer money for our grief
and their guilt.
My hiccups echo as I think of our
one-in-a-million big gray tomcat
and poor widowed Alice,
waiting at home.
And I hate the pair of twenties
changing hands
and Dad's lifted mood.

I follow my father
as he leaves with a wave
instead of burning down their house
like I wanted.

Daddy's Girl

My father does not see me
through the wave of alcohol.
The tide rises and falls.
I am wading alone ankle deep.

Unexpectedly, the surf subsides
just enough
Dad raises his head,
the texture of the couch
branded on his cheek.

The red veins in his eyes
emphasize the green as he
looks me up and down.

"Wow," he says. "You really have gotten big."
        Muffled words
aimed directly at my ass
            crash over,

pull me under, I
want to disappear, standing

in tight pink sweatpants with my
stomach and thighs and butt, because Daddy
just saw me, and he said I'm fat.

Slasher

Mom makes him say **sorry.**
I tell him
it's okay.
I don't mind,
but it is **not**
and I **do**.
Want to cut something
with a grunt,
grab my pen,
slice words into my diary,
press so hard they are engraved
on a week's worth of days.

I WILL BE THIN

One Year Diary

The Art of War

Map out what I will eat
down to each nibble.

Day one
I implement the Plan.

Day two
Eat the same rations.

Day three   Day four
Won't alter what seems to be working.

Do not deviate from
the Plan.

Gaining ground by losing pounds.
You can survive on so little.

Day five   Day six
Week one   Week two

I march on, begin to make progress
slimming down, achieving victory

executing my Plan of Attack
against my sworn enemy: FAT.

"Na Na Hey Hey Kiss Him Goodbye"

The moon
shines its face.
The riptide sweeps my father away.
He does not look back, does not
see me making changes,

                  necessary changes,
                        doing better.

It's okay to look now, Daddy,

                  getting thinner.

I promise to be good. Please
see me, make me okay. Daddy, come back.
I-love-you-I-

           hate-you-I-don't-give-a-shit.

Go ahead disappear
drown in your vice
I will be fine

                 you will be thin

I will be here

waiting.

Unreliable Narrator

It is actually not so much
the *moon* that sweeps
my father away as it is
a coven of Al-Anon women
who surround my mother
and chant that
she is fully capable
of supporting herself
time to cast out
her unemployed alcoholic.

We're all doing it,
they whisper
a hex
on Mom.

Al-Anon ex-wives
dressed like Stevie Nicks
dancing together
at The Crossbow Lounge
where my mother
enchants,

proving she can still bewitch
with a spell or two
of her own.

Miss Diagnosis

I break down in hysterical tears
the morning I realize
Dad took the blow-dryer
when Mom kicked him out.
Sobbing, I grip
the cupboard door,
one hand covering my mouth,
as I stare at the space
where the Conair should be
my hair dripping cold and
silent around my shoulders.

Mom announces
I'm not actually upset
about the blow-dryer.
Proudly points out I'm *really* reacting
to my father leaving
        displaced emotion
        Psychology 101,
        her education in action.

Running fingers
through limp, wet strands,
I can admit
I'm super sad
about Dad leaving
to live on a friend's couch,
but as I squeeze water from clumped hair,
my grief is sharp and focused
on my unruly,
frizzy
day ahead.

Flood

The dam we've been depending on
that's been repaired time and again
mended with silver spools of delicate hope

BURSTS.

Mom is *such a bitch*
for not giving Dad
one more
final third chance.
"Your dad and I separating
has nothing to do with you," she tells me,
which is such a dipshit thing to say.
If it has nothing to do with me,
why
is it swinging me around by the neck?

Circus Pup

We adopt
a consolation prize,
with the adorable name, Cheers,
who must have come from the circus.
She leaps straight from the floor
into my arms.
Flips around and jumps again
if I hitch her hind legs just so.
One small
black-and-white furball
with floppy bangs
fills a whole hurting house
with laughter
and light.

Curling her soft self
into the safe crook of my neck
each night she sword swallows
all my darkest thoughts, until
they disappear.

She Houdinis herself
free from her harness
takes her magic act
across our long country road
where cars are rare
but fast
an escape artist
giving us thrills and chills.

Cara and Christopher dress her in
a sparkly pink tutu

that rustles as she runs
toward my outstretched arms
waiting to catch her.

Today's performance interrupted
when a wicked bike
swings to meet her
instead.
The speeding motorcycle
appears from thin air
sends her rolling
and rolling, leaves her
still and bleeding.

My talented girl's final trick
incomplete
because I mistimed
her cue
when I called.

The Minnow

My shattered heart longs
to comfort
Cara and Christopher,
sit them down
explain all the leaving
so they
can hurt less
but I don't understand it
myself
and can't seem to stop
feeling so helpless.

One clear Saturday afternoon
Mom is off Jazzercising;
eleven-year-old Cara
lies on her bed, light
streaming through her window.
I walk in and quietly say, "Hey."
She turns, pleading with
shipwreck-eyes. I
run to give her a hug attack,
and we both start crying.

Soon Chris drifts by
in Spider-Man pajamas
nothing needs to be said,
we shift on the bed.
Make room for him
in our life raft embrace.

The sunbeam's fingers
stroke our hair, Strawberry Shortcake
watches from Cara's pillowcase,
and we stay
sobbing   bobbing
sobbing   bobbing
      for a long time.

But it isn't enough

we are

        lost.

The Island

Dad is done sleeping on couches,
takes off to New York to pursue
his drinking career because, Mom says,
"Reality is too much for some people."

But I think in Dad's case,
      Reality just isn't enough.

We are left incomplete, yet remarkably
afloat.

When the worst happens,
at least there's no more worrying
about the worst.
      ~wisdom from Judy Blume

That sensation of holding our breath
preparing for the monsoon
to pull us under, is gone,
replaced with the forecast
that nothing will ever
      everevereverevereverever
be quite okay again.

I don't talk about it
only eat less,
turning it inward
on myself.

Making sure no one
gets hurt by my
RAGE.

Break Up 2

My best friend Samantha
and my Jonathan
are now an official "going together" couple.
I'm happy for them really
        just a little embarrassed
        that one time I misunderstand and think
        we're all heading to the mall
        to hang out
        after church,
        but it's actually a
        date-sort-of-thing of just them.

Perfect together,
a flawless matched set
with their good grades
and big brains. Unbroken families,
        every version of success
        bursting out
        of their shiny clean asses.
I'm happy for them. Really.

The Diet 2

I chant to my reflection
>You do not need anybody.
>You do not need anything.
>
>Don't even need food.
>You are not allowed to need.
>
>Need is weakness

look myself in the eye
>and you will never be weak again.

Cutting-Room Floor

I'm surprised
my movie-loving father
doesn't ask
for even partial custody.

No *Kramer v. Kramer*
cinematic confrontation.
No declaration
of *Irreconcilable Differences*.
No hashing out
the dirty details
        in some dramatic courtroom
        battle scene.
Dad gives us up
not a *mention* of visiting rights
let alone a fight.

Then again,
what sort of homelife
could he provide?
Mom says he's taken up residence
at a bar in New York
called Ray's Inn.

That seven-hour drive
would probably make it hard
for us to get to school on time anyway.

The Wail

I open my mouth wide
scream with all my strength
yet no one

         stops

               slows down

                       or even turns my way

for they have not heard
a peep
out of me.

Reviews Are In

"Wow."

      "You've lost weight, haven't you?"

    "You look great!"

        "I cannot believe how much willpower you have."

"Amazing!"

I bask in waves of awe
all
encouraging me to go on.

Brownie? Psyche!

You do not need to eat   you are above
eating
Eating is for the weak   the needy
not you,
strong-willed one.

It's not that I don't like food.
Oh how I would enjoy
scarfing down
right about now.

But don't you dare
forsake your mission.

. . . so hungry all the time . . .

I succumb
a tiny bite of brownie
not low-fat
not sugar-free
definitely not
made with carob.
Immediately
spit
the chocolate lusciousness
into a napkin.
A brown glob of shame spreads
turning napkin clear with
grease and spit
until I bury it
deep in the trash.
Confirm my dedication.

See? That brownie was not
so irresistible
after all.

The willpower I possess
could change the whole world.
Or at least change one body,
mine.

Rapture by Blondie

I'm not the most skilled student driver
in driver's ed,
but I'm the one willing
to drive back from the ice-cream stand.
The only one not eating ice cream.

Everyone whines
about wearing seat belts,
required thanks to new laws
and crash test dummy
slapstick commercials.
But I like the way
the taut band snugs
smooth across my flat belly.

I inherit Dad's
primer-gray Chrysler Cordoba.
The cheap replacement
for that wrecked company car.
Mom says nobody drives in NY
plus he's never
getting his license back, anyway.

It doesn't take me long
to understand
our curling country roads
are made for speed,
that tilting back the seat
and blasting my mixtape
makes me feel like my nasty,
ashtray-scented, fifteen-ton car
sets me free.

Runner-Up 2

Mom is so popular
with her Al-Anon friends.
Every night is Ladies' Night
for a lady with her looks,
and "going out dancing"
is her new favorite sport.

She dates
while I babysit with
bitterness,
giving rides to soccer practice while
Mom plays the field.
Sweet sixteen, my ass.
I'm living in the shadow
of a thirty-four-year-old divorcée.

Best years of my life, *like hell.*
Everything's bullshit.

I wouldn't mind having
one of those ordinary-looking mothers
without lives of their own,
who live for their daughters
instead of borrowing their clothes.

See Me

Others obsessed with
my bones
ask,

           "How did you do it?"
        "What's your secret?"
     "Can I shrink too?"

Annoying comments
on my eating habits:
compulsive chewing,
consuming so slowly,
the sameexactthing
day after day
rice cakes
and apples
safe foods that
won't tempt me overboard,
won't make me fat.

Even Mom notices,
is so proud
of my willpower.

Mr. Mortimer
stops me in the hallway
uses my nickname
"Miss New York,"
from my I ♥ NY essays.
Clutching a fat manila file
pregnant with papers
he patiently asks,

"You doing okay?"
with genuine concern
I cannot allow

his question to sink
in; my smile screams too
loud that "everything's great!"
       don't want
       you to care.
block his concern
with a nod and a
"yes" and a
"see you in class."
       Please don't worry about me.
       Your worry
       will make me weak.

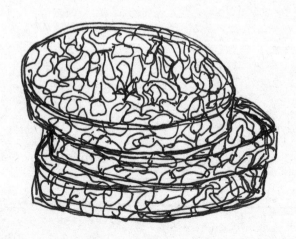

Master and Commander

Half an hour
to eat an orange
so careful,
teeth worrying over
every
tiny
capsule of pulp.

Forty-five minutes
to eat a rice cake.
Tongue slowly melting
synthetic modules to paper that sticks
on the roof of my mouth.

One hour to eat
a chicken breast sandwich
grilled   *obviously.*
Leave the roll and chew
each sour filament
into dry oblivion.

                              Stay in charge,

I restrain my craving
lower my voice
hold everything in
stingy
and secure.

                    Have all power. All authority.
                              Total control.

The Victor

My clothes
once tight
are loose.

I love it.

Hide my beautiful new self
in folds of fabric
luxuriate in the glory of
                    taking up less space.

                Meek and delicate
                    quiet and small.

Volume Control

I don't care
about fashion anymore
but do have favorite looks.
A pink hooded tee
with three-quarter sleeves
that floats
on my shoulder blade hangers.
Delicious dark wash denim
with zero pudge overflow.
High-waisted sweatpants
tied tight to defy gravity.
My signature
ample green sweatshirt
my NY uncle
got me from his job at Perrier.
And underneath it all,

a skintight leotard daily.
It holds me in,
defines my edges,
                    Keeps you from oozing out.
makes me feel safe and secure
like a little girl.

Poor Loser

Mom and I drive the kids
to New York,
roaring we are *independent women*
with untested map-reading skills,
but we get across Pennsylvania,
through the city, over
Brooklyn Bridge to Queens,
driving east
right past Granny's house,
through Nassau and Suffolk counties
wind up in Patchogue,
an hour past our destination
       long after most
             would've quit going.

When we finally stop at a pay phone,
get directions, turn around, backtrack,
walk in Granny's front door,
Lucy is so
envious
because I won our competition
       by a lot.

That must be why
she accuses me of being glassy-eyed

and clumsier than usual
       I do step on her feet an awful lot.
says I'm way too thin thin thin
       Wasn't that the whole point?
warns everyone something's wrong with me.
       As if she wouldn't trade places in a second.

So now I'm reaping uneasy looks,
family focusing on me.
Mom's pride in my willpower
starts to slip, and I
want to point out
that Ray's Inn
is just around the corner.

My father
so close
yet gone in a way that is
worse than mine.

Big Sister

A milk chocolate bunny
sweats and softens in a small pot on the stove
as I help Christopher make chocolate-covered
pretzels, chips, marshmallows, crackers, and
everything edible we can dip in chocolate.
Carefully, I interview him as he samples the results.

Don't you dare take a single taste,
just smell it all deeply.

I hold the chocolate so close to my face,
almost touching my lips,
take a meditative inhale
allow it to fill the top of my throat
with a suede waft of fruity cocoa.

Can smelling such luxury make you fat?

This is fun for Chris,
his self-absorbed older sister
whose dry sense of humor
matches his own
fully present, focusing all her attention on him.
I grow annoyed when he claims to be full,
and he obligingly
eats for me.

Revenge of the Nerd

I turn down invitations to hang out with
the other kickline girls.
Still a Sequinette, and love our long, grueling practices, but
my aim isn't popularity anymore. It's infamy.

>   *Mustn't miss your*
>   *dinner routine.*

My meager meal grows cold as I
mash nude strands of spaghetti with my teeth
until it runs liquid
down my throat.

Chased by a vigorous walk
burning calories
dragging Cara and Christopher along,
        another sibling bond
            born of my obsession.
A mile up the road to 7-Eleven
to buy penny gum
by the dollar

scoring snaps of sweetness
to beat back my hunger
the raging tiger

>   *must be*
>   *subdued with tricks.*

Smelling, chewing
drinking water
brushing teeth
sleeping as much as possible,
chairs and whips
I wield
        to tame
            my Hunger.

Off with Her Head

Sometimes I feel
everyone watching me
so intently
I forget how to walk naturally
across the vast stage that is
the school cafeteria.
According to the psychology class notes
in Mother's voice,
it's just my "invisible audience"
most adolescents share.
Theoretically,
we're all
too worried about ourselves
to watch each other that closely,
but it sure feels like I'm
on constant display.

Those imagined spectators
materialize into actual stares
from all corners of the lunchroom
as the most popular girl in school
approaches.
> *Release the ceremonial doves.*

Summoned before teen royalty,
under the echoing clatter of sporks, I can
practically hear the murmurs and gasps.
She asks me how I lost so much weight
and I am pleased to describe my regimen,
yet murderously annoyed
at having it interrupted.

Reading Hour

I am thinking about food
all the time
don't know when it started
how it happened
what it implies, but I can't focus
on any of that right now.

I'm busy looking through Mom's
illustrated cookbook
at all the glorious food
so beautifully photographed
I can almost smell it.

I flip through
an entire meal.
Appetizers, sides,
        main dishes,
and my favorite genre,
           desserts.
Saving the sexy climax
for the back of the book.

A flower-shaped tart blinks
demurely from the title page.
Cakes stand defiantly,
gaping wedges removed,
their round perfection
wrecked
by someone else's weakness.

Here is the bundt
drawn round herself
icing dripping down her back.
Cookies gather boldly
on china plates,
chocolate chip
      peanut butter
            shortbread
                sugar.
Each a familiar character with a backstory
and evil motive all its own.

Pencil-sharpener curls
of milk chocolate,
so precise,
I lose myself
contemplating a single matte shaving.
The pages consume me.

I feel so ultra special knowing
I can resist it all.

Forget classic literature.
There's nothing
quite like curling up with
The Good Housekeeping Illustrated Cookbook.

A Room of Her Own

My bedroom is
my refuge
shelter
strength.
There I exist
hour after hour
reading weight-loss schemes
replenishing my resolve.

Daydreaming
          no longer
          about boys
but about eating,
mind
consumed by food.

I use fingers
          no longer
          for private play
but for gauging
wrists
calves
thighs
waist.

Testing stomach:

                              flat enough?

Mirror image:

                              thin enough?

Manage those bones:

                    protrude enough?

No longer dieting,
I am the diet.
Becoming less each day.

My faded ink drawings
hang, watching weakly.

My head buzzes
high and hungry.

Slowly and deliberately
outside my walls

life happens.

Empty Sky

I feel
like I'm back
on that way high dive
so alone
uncertain
how to get off.

Hesitating,   I look
 for a way to land.

There is nowhere safe
no one to take my hand
or catch me
and the water looks so dark
and so deep.
I'll just hover here
on wings of Starvation.

Boy Toy

Mom's steady stream of suitors
has been a sad cornucopia of
soccer coaches and divorcés.
But now she wears
a dreamy look
in her fake green eyes,
like the world is filled with
brand-new colors.
Like *she's* the hormonal teen in the house.

I meet her new boyfriend for the first time
the two of them washing her black Buick
and his white convertible
in the driveway.
She says, "Hi." And he says, "Hi,"
and I walk by
like they're both invisible.

Lewis is like
if Elvis had a thick mustache
and a Pittsburgh accent;
he's twelve years younger
than Mom,
six older than me.

He accepts the challenge of
my surly silence,
preteen Cara's
icy stare,
and is moved
by Christopher,
the ten-year-old boy

who runs lightning fast
beside the other boys
because he doesn't have a bike,
and who never got taught how to catch a ball
properly,
and whose wide, father-famished eyes follow
Lewis everywhere.

The Boss

Mom laughs more.
Her *hear me roar* independence
fades to background noise
as she
starts to count on Lewis
instead of herself.
Instead of me.

Lewis
and I disagree a lot.
Mom takes his side,
blinded by bouquets of fresh flowers and
our first ever microwave oven he brings.

My life ruined by his random
unbreakable rules and insistence I learn
to mow the lawn,
cook the family a meal not from a can,
and clean up that
disgusting pigsty of a bedroom
        for Christ's sake.

At twenty-three,
starting his own
construction business,
Lewis tells my mother
to stop collecting
thick bricks of
government cheese
delights her with
romantic dates
to the supermarket.

Seduces my family
with white convertible car rides,
tickets to the Penguins
It's a hockey night in Pittsburgh!
and—ultimate local luxury—
a day at Kennywood,
home of the Thunderbolt.

Cara and Chris weaken
despite my firm coaching,
"Nobody is allowed to like Lewis."
          Must stay loyal to Dad.

But I find myself
lured
by Lewis's endless stacks
of vintage Marvel comics,
his vast collection
of movies recorded
from TV onto VHS and
an actual VCR to play them.

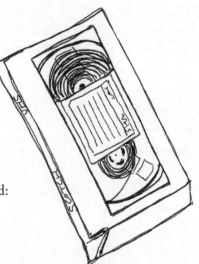

Finally, he shows his unbeatable hand:
tickets for five
to a Born in the U.S.A.
Bruce Springsteen concert.

Grudgingly, I concede,
"Lewis might not be so bad."

Renovation

A waist-high ceramic pig
wearing overalls
appears on our front lawn;
we can afford whimsy now.
A basketball hoop in the driveway
a pair of young mallard ducks
make a home of our creek.
We name them Bob and Anna.
They come waddling when we call
because Lewis can tame anything.

He builds an arched wooden bridge
to the wild back acres of our yard
buys Christopher a quad
to zoom past
his friends on bicycles.
Cara's dreams—a Swatch watch and J.Crew wardrobe
come true,
and for me
a breathtaking brand-new
portable electric Brother typewriter
to write without
spraining fingers
on Mom's clunky manual one.

Lewis loves rhyming wordplay
corny puns, teasing quips
decidedly *dad* humor.
        Unlike Dad, who
        at a school performance
        leaned over during a kid's

solo rendition of
'"Does Anybody Really Know What Time It Is?"
and ~~whispered~~,
"Will somebody give this kid
the fucking time already?"

Lewis works endlessly
building his business
is ambitious in ways
our father is not.
In one week,
still grimy from work,
he builds a basement fireplace
converting an unfinished square hole
brick
by solid brick

transforming
useless cinder block space
into a family room.

Welcome Back, Kotter

My father does not like
someone taking up
with the family he left

finishing the projects
he always meant
to get around to.

He comes back
moves into the house
and refuses to leave.

Comic Relief

Mom is furious
calls her lawyer and
flees with the kids to Lewis's
small apartment
outside Pittsburgh.

It's summer break,
and she wants me to come, but
Sequinette practice is starting
and I'm excited about
needing a smaller skirt
and being a senior
       but mostly about the smaller skirt.
I don't mind staying.

Dad's always been a happy drunk
and he's kind of drunk all the time now.

Says, "Holy cow," I look great.
Is *so proud* of me for losing so much weight.
Introduces me to a pretty young brunette
with makeup spackled thickly over her acne
who drapes herself around his neck like
he belongs to her.

Dad can't get over
how wonderfully thin I am,
doesn't give me shit about
skipping meals
or my Kellogg's Special K dinners.
We stay up late,
hang out on the couch

watching *Carson*, *SNL*, and *Cosby*.
Zero percent of Lewis's rules,
in fact, we mock the chore chart together.
Although when it's time to wake up to
scout for a job,
I begin to suspect
the coolest people to hang out with
maybe don't make the best dads.

Nightmare

I wake to a noise,
            from deep in the basement.
A muffled metallic
            clank *clank* *clank*

I must wake Dad.
            Something bad is happening.
Someone bad is in the house.

But nobody could sleep
through that sound.
Not even Dad.
Even tired or
drunk. I hear a grunt,

            an anguished yell

and realize

that horrible sound
the someone bad in the house

is Dad.

Clues in the Basement

I start praying,
listen intently as Dad
comes upstairs with a groan and
squeaks the mattress hard
just once
and goes silent.

I can't sleep.
I can't sleep.
I can't sleep.

I channel my inner Nancy Drew
boldly crawl out of bed
slip quietly down the stairs
past our names engraved
in the cement foundation
find *The Mystery of the Smashed Fireplace.*
The first clue:
            chipped hunks of brick.
Look, another clue:
            a rusty axe leaning
            against the wall.
I slide
arms tight
around my faded yellow
sleep shirt emblazoned with
the false claim I am "Super Chick."
I extend
one
cold
finger.

Trace it through brick dust
caked thick
on the blunt blade.

I turn to stone.

My father's broken brain
has coated our new family room
in chunks of broken brick.

I reason
Dad must be so drunk he
doesn't know what he's doing.

But the next night
when the steady
　　　clank *clank* *clank*
starts up again,
I pray this new
violent version
of drunk dad
knows *exactly* what he's doing
and that he keeps what he's doing
downstairs.

Alateen

Dad heads back to
Ray's Inn, NY,
becomes what Mom calls
an "active alcoholic"
and stops calling,
even on some birthdays.

Lewis, furious
about the fireplace,
paces the basement
with such rage I fear
all the walls will crumble into dust.

I downplay the axe incident.
Mom already feels guilty
for leaving me.

Lewis fixes the fireplace
the ducks, Bob and Anna, come back
and Mom takes us to Alateen
where other kids
talk openly about their alcoholic parents.
Like it's okay
to *say* all this stuff.

It's a backwards, opposite day
bizzaro world where
we only discuss
things I can never talk about.

Like how the people
who are supposed to protect us
sometimes can't
or don't.
Painful family secrets are exposed
actual feelings rendered into words.
Impressed by the proceedings
I open my mouth, share my
axe-dad story. Even joke about
The Shining but confess
how freaked out I was. *Terrified.*
The other kids of alcoholics
stare at me with round eyes.

When we leave,
I carry a lit lantern.
The dark basement
less lonely,
its dangerous pull
weakened.

But Mom is busy with her
new counseling gig
on top of her teaching job
plus planning a
brand-new fresh start wedding with Lewis
and doesn't bring us back,
which is probably for the best
since I shared too much anyway.

Seething

My anger,
my loudness
my craving that I've been holding in
controlling
denying starts to seep out
not in slow, small portions but
all   at   once.

Flaring like a blowtorch
out of control
scorching those in my path.
Lewis and I battle
constantly over my
mowing the grass half-assed,
taking sloppy phone messages,
and not rewinding the VHS tapes.
He hates ~~me~~ my habit
of staying up late
having no energy all day,
and the way my temper
snaps like a rubber band aimed at
Cara and Christopher, who seem so
spoiled and annoying now.

One morning Lewis
storms into my room,
lifts me from bed,
carries me down the hallway
and dumps me directly
into the bathtub.
Promises, "The next time you

try sleeping past eleven,
that shower will be on."

Mom imagines
"what the neighbors must think."
Our sweet house
all its extra windows releasing
screams, hollers, and
door *SLAMs*!

The ghosts of our brand-new start
haunting us.

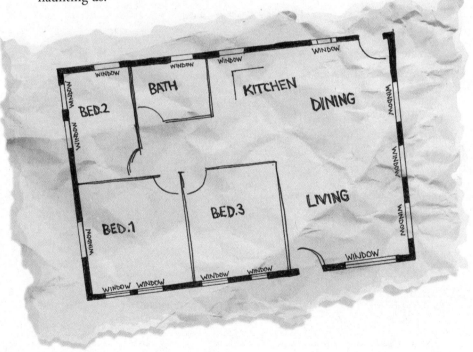

Scape Girl

Mom looks
from psychology journals to me
asking leading questions.
I try to answer
right, never admit to
hunger,
repeat my catchphrase,
I just ate,
I just ate,
I just ate.

                    You don't deserve to eat.

She cannot learn
my hunger
is my source of power.

                    Control your appetite, bitch.

Despite this,
Mom announces
I'm anorexic.

                    Anorexic? You wish!

But I am obsessed with food.
I can't be anorexic.

Mom thinks she's solved everything.
All of the problems
are mine.

Mommy Dearest

Caring and comforting,
talking to me
in her condescending "counselor voice."
I *feel* like being left alone.

Mom goads me to the bathroom scale
so she can check.
I submit with fingers
privately pressing
up against the waist-high towel-rack
forcing numbers higher
to get Mom off my back.

She cries helplessly
when I   will   not   taste
the diet birthday cake
she baked special for me.

A halo of fresh strawberries smile amiably
from their spongy, round bed.
I inhale its sweet scent instead.
She must be so jealous now
I'm thinner than her.

The Bird

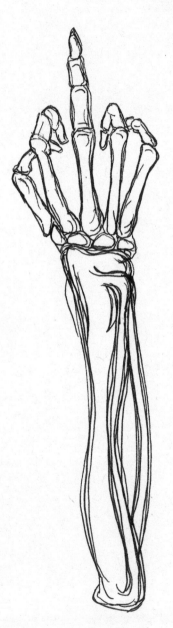

This body
is a
hard
numb
ruthless
middle finger
flipped
at the world.

The Ultimate Act
of Passive Aggression

Just

      shrink

            away.

Borderline

Sitting in social studies
zoned out
doodling. Calculating
how much weight I have lost. Testing
how it looks in dashes and slashes
clumps of five pounds.
Sophisticated charts marking progress.
      I actually am good at math.
Greasy Mr. Groth is passing back tests
when I stand, the edges of my vision fill
with black snow, darkness
fighting
        to the front of my eyes, threatening.

Oh crap—head heavy
room moving

I sit back down quick, hugging my paper
sweating despite being cold.
That was close.

With a sly smile, I
turn my attention back
to my weight loss
numbers.

Stray

My Body
wants to help me
survive this fake famine
slows everything down
making it harder to lose

doesn't understand
the whole point of not eating.

My Body
is pissing me off
like a puppy dog trying to please
but getting it wrong

getting in the way.

Why can't it behave
sit
stay
roll over

play dead.

Quit trying to help
stop licking my face

just   go   away.

Duck, Duck, Fuck

Our gentle ducks
are both hit by one car
like the driver
was hunting them.
Bob survived,
his beak ripped off
gleaming green mallard head bobbing
stumbling
in circles of grief
and confusion
around the splayed feathers of his
dear dead wife, Anna.
A beakless Daffy
after a run-in with Elmer Fudd,
but with none of the loony humor.
No snapping that beak back in place.
Lewis forced to have the vet "take care of him"
and all of us
seeped in regret
for ever loving anything so fragile.

Sequinettes 2

In the back of the bus
with the other seniors
for an hour ride
to encourage
football players to
"Whippa Alliquippa"
we discover
I am the ONLY ONE
who knows
every single word
to the Foreigner song
"Juke Box Hero."
Hairbrush mic
passed to my hand
my name chanted
until I belt out
the most earnest, off-key solo,
Gotta keep on rockin'!
All go wild, and belonging feels
so much better
than being closed
away in my room.

My bus seat squeaks
as I drop back down.
My sister Sequinettes cheer.
My grin stays put
as my seatmate gives my back

a slap of praise
but my mind panics,
flies home to dwell on
beloved ducks,
now buried in our
ever-expanding pet cemetery.

This "Juke Box Hero" moment
is nice but
much too fragile to hold onto.

Nightmare 2

I wake up
springs of my bed biting my bones
clothed in sweat, shaking from a dream
that I ate.

What! Why! No!
The hell?

Breathing in heavy panic,
I slide a hand across my stomach
check my hip bookends
relax, everything's okay.

It was all just a dream.

Fall Out

Standing in the shower
dialed to scalding,
the only time I feel warm
so cold lately, always so cold.

I'm happily lost in hot, wet embrace
warming my popsicle core

lean my head into the stream,
hands through hair
something tickles my palms.
I look at fingers cradling a tangled web of
long brown strands.

Fear's icy knife stabs through
my warm reverie.

Climax

I sit in church
stained glass rays
of red and
blue and yellow dance
against the grain of the pew.

Waiting to
break bread together
body of Christ
blood of our Lord.

I appreciate He
sweat
       bled
             died
for me.
I do.

But all I hear is
        Jesus, how many calories
           in a sliver of bread?
           a swallow of wine?

Friendless Haiku

Month by month by month
My period a no show
Lucky, lucky me

Scatterbrain

I can't

concentrate

on anything

for long;

GONE

HUNGRY

Kid You Not

My hair is brittle and thin.
I'm forever cold to my core.

Weird peach fuzz grows
all over my skin
my body's pathetic attempt
to hold heat.
It hurts to sit for long
on this jutting less-blasphemous butt.

My clothes hang from
boney hips and shrunken breasts.
Even my Jordache jeans
are loose.

Jelly shoes
grow too large,
hard ground jars
through the clear, smelly plastic.
Sunken eyes stare with
decreased depth perception.
I pinball off walls and people,
lacking the vigor to avoid them,
    a zombie,
    not from *Thriller* . . .
    from *Night of the Living Dead.*
I am hollow. Alone.

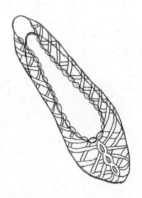

But my *real* problem?
           Your REAL problem!

My determination to stay
starving
is tired and weak.
My metabolism sooo slooooow,
my weight loss
stops.

Three / The Incredible Growing Girl

Go Tell It on the Mountain

The elderly, homebound
members of our church
sometimes request
a bit of help,
instead get
our youth group
goofing around
inside their house,
pretending to scrub
floors and windows.

But now
we're taking our "help" crew
on the road.
Heading south
to West Virginia.
Joining teens
from all over.
Our first big mission trip.

We stand shoulder to shoulder
in the church lobby on Sunday
asking for sponsors.
Wallets and checkbooks open fast.
Everyone feels good
sending young people
off to bless the less fortunate,
to be the hands and feet of Jesus.

~~My~~ Jonathan
and Samantha so delighted
with each other they're
~~killing me~~
annoying to be around.

But this trip promises
to be an adventure
meeting other young people
who love Jesus too.
Besides,
West Virginia
sounds far away and
exotic,
like a place
I can be anyone I want.

Habitat for Humans

The worksites are
cracked and broken log-cabin homes
with two-story-high satellite dishes
planted in the dirt and nothing
in the fridge besides beer.

The wide gaping *want*
is physically manifested
in the form of dirt-smudged children
following us
barefoot in the heat,
eating our packed sandwiches of
peanut butter and honey.

We get real
about working
try to beat back the need
with hammers
caulk guns
and compassion.

Time off is spent
playing chicken in the pool
with boys from faraway places like
Indiana and Illinois.
We flirt and pray together,
sing hope-filled songs
around the campfire.

I never want to leave
even eat a few of those
honey and peanut butter
sandwiches myself
because I am too present
alive
and grateful
to remember

      ~~your ultimate goal~~.

As the days pass
I barely feel
the steel trap of guilt
snapping at me, hardly hear that
desperate inner-voice
screaming

     ~~"you worthless pigbitch"~~

drowned out
as I sing and play and help.

Payback

Home, I add
an afternoon snack
to my rigid food plan.
One teaspoon of peanut butter.
Protein
to stop hair
from falling out.

I can deal with dark circles
and grim-reaper cheeks
but balding?
Not a look I think I can pull off.

Thick, sweet
peanutty paste
coats my mouth
and loosens the spell.
I stay in control
until day four when

my resolve
          dissolves.

Without warning,
brain urging
hurry up hurry up hurry up
until
I'm rationalizing spoonful
number five.

Panic

I stop the automatic pilot,
take back the controller,
                    drop the spoon, Miss,
                        and step away
                            from that jar

hear
the taunts
of the lumps of peanut butter
        swimming in me

working out of control
        to make me   FAT
Fat   Fat   FAT
                        Fat   Fat
            Fat   fat
    fat   Fat   fat
                                Fat
                    FAT   Fat
    Fat   FAT
Fat

Fat   Fat   FAT
                    Fat   Fat
        Fat   fat
    fat   Fat   fat
                            Fat
        FAT   Fat
    Fat   FAT   Fat
Fat   Fat   FAT
    Fat   Fat
        Fat   fat
    fat   Fat   fat

Penance

I immediately go jogging
try to run out
of myself
out of this body,
its greed and need.

What have you done?

I am desperate
to go back to Before,
deduct
five fatty spoonfuls
sitting stubbornly in my stomach

which is now cramping
I dry heave
in the parched grass
beside the road.

*Quick, quick, quick
get it all out out out.*

I am raw and retching
but too weak to lift the
heavy peanut butter from my gut.

You are a failure at this too.

Cars whiz by
someone may
see me,
so my body must absorb

all your sin.

Rebound Effect

According to
the laws of motion,

        every action

has an equal
and opposite

        reaction.

            Fucking science!

My body
starving
for months
now forces me to   EAT.

          Absolute anarchy!

I grasp and grab
at my program
of control,
but my body
makes up
for lost time
pressuring me
to binge
determined brain
accounting for
every

        hungry

moment
my

                ever
             expanding

body
endured

Vicious hungry vacuum

Bringing
the universe
back
into
balance.

your ass now a planet

Damn you, Newton!

Wheels of the Bus

Each day
I try to get
back on schedule
try to stop
eating so much
But no matter how firm
my determination
I eventually
eat-out-of-control
you Loser
I hate myself
and resolve
to do better
and do
for a time
and then break down

eat again
you're Disgusting
I hate myself
am weak
must break this cycle
stop eating
always fail
always eat
what is Wrong with you?
I hate myself
just want
to stop
but cannot
I Hate you
And I hate myself.

Va-Va-Voom

My edges blur and I am absolutely
out of my mind
over **losing my focus**.

At the kitchen counter
Mom looks me up and down,
tells me, "Okay, honey,
you have put on
the right amount of weight.
You can **stop gaining now**."

And I smile weakly
run to my room
close myself inside,
dive on my bed and
weep because
I know I
can't.

The Guzzler

My clothes
once loose
are tight

                    hate this

forced to show myself
in the stretch and pucker of fabric
embarrassed by my body

                    taking up too much space

swollen and full
big and loud.

Gloaters

I dread seeing others
that first time.

Stop hearing
"You look great."
Instead, met by prying eyes,

exploring my body
invading my shame
lingering longest
on areas most changed.

                    My dear!
            What a fat ass you have!

Some seem warmer,
wickedly happy I failed.
Some are disgusted
by my new state.
Some
appear relieved to have me back,
sent spiraling to *chunky town*
on my big fat fanny.

And I
loathe   them   all.

I'll make it yet
I silently challenge
wait and see
just wait and see.

Random Survivor Tips from Teachers

Dear Children:
If you find yourself caught
in quicksand
sinking
do whatever it takes
to get horizontal
move as little as possible
so you will sink slower
and increase odds
of being rescued.

Dear Students:
If you find yourself captured
by a python
squeezed and squeezed
till your eyes nearly pop
you must pinch
that snake hard
pythons famously hate
being pinched
and if you pinch hard enough
it will drop to the ground
and leave you alone.

Dear Females:
If you find yourself attacked
by a rapist
rake your nails across his eyes
punch his throat
knee his groin.

Although, be warned that
resisting the rape may escalate things,
and you could get yourself murdered,
also be mindful,
you really shouldn't scream
because that's what he wants.
And try not to call out, "rape!"
Instead, yell, "fire!"
because if you shout "rape!"
nobody will come to help you.

Pink Tulle

Mom lets me
pick bridesmaids' dresses
from the pastel offerings
in a JCPenney catalog.

A month before her wedding
I'll be wearing
that "timeless elegance"
satin dress to the prom
since it costs three times
my most expensive jeans and
it's silly to buy two dresses.
Especially since
I'm going to the prom with
some random red-haired guy
from study hall
who asked me,
after a tall underclassman
turned me down.
> Rejected
> despite offering
> to pick him up in
> Lewis's white convertible
> since the sophomore doesn't drive yet.
Caring about my prom dress
at this point
would be pathetic.

Not that the shiny pink monstrosity
that arrives in the mail
could be mistaken for anything
but sad.
Stiff and bridesmaid-looking
it barely resembles the polished ad
and grips my growing waist
like a shimmering pink python
that clashes with my date's mullet.

At the Prom

Random red-haired guy
bores me
with a monologue about BMX bikes.
I flee to lip-sync to Prince
on the dance floor
with the other Sequinettes,
and later sneak
to the darkest corner of the balcony,
where I impulsively kiss
a friend who's had a
not-so-secret, secret crush on me.
I flirt with anyone
but my date
pretend to sleep
the forty-minute
ride home,
magically waking
as we pull into my driveway.
Before I can escape,
random red-haired guy
from study hall
who rescued me
from going to prom alone says,
"We'll talk Monday."
I know we won't

because right now,
being randomly cruel
simply because I can
gives me a feeling I like.

Fallout

The friend
I kissed
shows up
the next morning.
      I had no idea
      he knew where I lived.
When I open the door
he falls through
clings to me
like he's been drowning.

I'm forced to decide
if it's better
to be honest
and confess our kiss
was only a tasty diversion
from BMX bikes
or see how this feels.

He is
smart and sarcastic,
cute in an oddball way
but likes me so much more
than I like myself.

I take the path
of least resistance.
We date.

He does
such nice things for me
installs speakers

in my Cordoba
and gives me back rubs
until his hands are so tired
he has to ask
if I mind if he stops.

I let him unbutton my oxford
as we kiss in his elderly parents' den
after their bedtime.
He is *good* at kissing,
but I block any move
to unhook my bra
my twin elbow goalies
guarding bloated breasts.
He doesn't even try
my Jordaches.

Maybe because they're
tight again.

Blondie Jr.

In the drugstore
I pause at a wall
of blond boxes
watching me
sending me backward in time to
Granny's smoky-yellow kitchen.

I tingle with
that old ache
for magicical transformation.

Ambitious, I pick
a honey-blond beauty,
bring her home to help.

Pulling on
plastic gloves,
my eyes yelp

at the sharp scent of ammonia.
I combine potions,
ignore instructions.

Slather my head
with burning elixir
sit, face squinched
dabbing flaming drips
as I've seen Mom do
so often.

This sour expression
never pictured on the box.

Finally,
I wash away the stringy brown
and unveil a new neon shade
radiant tangerine!

Not a quitter,
I repeat, get
highlighter yellow!

My hair, now
brittle, starts
shedding in the shower again,
but the pale strands
never show.
Just tickle my palms
while water
flows through my fingers.

Glass Houses

Another Sequinette
is shrinking
to a fraction of her former self.
Everyone is concerned,
talking behind her dwindling back.

". . . way too thin . . ."
"Those leggings weren't baggy before."
"Did you see her eat anything today?"

That should be me,
used to be me.
And I'm a big jelly apple.

You are too weak.

So despite the fact
I've been in   her shoes
swimming on bony feet,
I have no help to offer.
She should be helping me

get back
to that island of starvation.

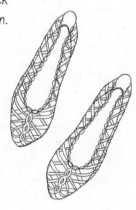

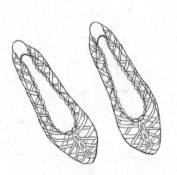

Wedding of the Century

Mom makes the most beautiful
bright and shining bride
at a picturesque church
we've never been to on Sunday.

And the two
shall become ~~one~~ five.

At the dance party reception, I'm glad
I broke up with my friend-turned-boyfriend
  who cried
   despite my crisp yellow hair
because it turns out,
Lewis has some friends who are
   !!!!!!!!hothothot!!!!!!
One with a perfect crooked smile
flirts with me
I spin in his arms
to "Lady in Red"
my pink
"timeless elegance" monstrosity
red hot.
  Until Lewis
threatens dismemberment
if his friend doesn't leave
his "daughter" alone.

My handsome Prince Charming
leaves early
our happily ever after

over before it began.
    I guess
it'd be a *little* weird
to start rounding bases
with my new stepdad's
high school football buddy
but *hell* was he hot
and *damn* am I mad.

Duds

I try laxatives,
> *the lazy girl's purging tool.*

They are so unpredictable,
send me flying for bathrooms.

Give God-awful gas, *wasn't me*
burning diarrhea, *cha-cha-cha.*

Make me reek
as if something
crawled up my butt
and died.

But worst of all
the chocolate squares
of sweet wax
with an aftertaste

> *fail at the one thing*
> *you really need*

don't help me
lose weight.

Surgeon General's Loss

Smoking causes cancer
and according to Brooke Shields,
"Spoils your looks."
      I hate the way Dad
          smokes and quits and smokes again.
But rumor has it,
smoking can make you skinny.
                    to hell with pink lungs
                      you need thin thighs.

I sit down on the grass alone
with a pack of super-skinny slims
I hope will make me
      super-skinny
      slim.

I practice lighting up,
pretend I'm
an actress playing a role
      sophisticated heroine
      in black and white
      or heroin addict
      in Technicolor,
      trying to recapture the *magic*
      of my hollow-eyed stare.
I push past the burning,
the urge to cough,
pulling and squinting
until I imagine it looks cool.

But the puff-yourself-slim plan
doesn't work on me
and smoking is
just another
failed attempt
on my long list of
failed attempts
to lose weight.

Back to the Future

College tuition
isn't in the family budget
and due to my homework policy of *never*
my grades are *whatever*
aside from the writing ones.

Application deadlines
Woosh! by
my fleeting vision of
journalism school
      away
grounded
before it can even land
on a specific campus.

Lewis ~~forces~~ finds me a job
at his friend's dry cleaner
where I memorize the customers
by the sizes on their tags.

Mom helps me fill out
"we're poor please help" paperwork
for classes at
Butler County Community College
the old BC3 default plan
for underachievers.

Taste the Rainbow

I become "that misfit chick"
hanging around
the movie theater.
Raising Arizona, Fatal Attraction,
Throw Mama from a . . .
Planes, Trains, and Automobiles.
       "At the movies" is
       my favorite place to be.
Sprain my ankle while watching
Flashdance in the living room.
       Just another steel town girl
       on a Saturday night . . .
Write funny film reviews for the
Butler Beagle and fall in love
with an air force recruit,
two weeks before his
basic training in Texas.
He seals his promise to keep in touch
with a beautiful, bittersweet kiss.

       Time to really get in shape.
I am all about building muscle now.
BMI. Resting heart rate.
Cutting carbs.

I become "that misfit chick"
wearing turquoise scrunch socks
and yellow tights
doing the grapevine
in a purple leotard to "Jump"
at the aerobics studio
inside the mall.

Gradually,
my air force "boyfriend"
writes less
despite the rainbow cookies
I bake with Skittles
that bend all Mom's spatulas
and the high-quality
humor essays I craft
about running out of gas,
and grooming our new shelter dog
who loves chasing skunks and hates baths.

I try to copy Molly's cute
fuchsia Volkswagen
from *Pretty in Pink,*
paint my huge,
clunky Cordoba hot pink
using forty cans
of spray paint
leaving long pink drips down the doors
       it looks *great* in the rain.
Become "that misfit chick"
speeding around
in the ugly pink car
with clashing
burgundy interior
who cannot parallel park.

My colorful comedic essays
can't stop my air force crush
from disappearing.
     Everyone's a critic.
The aerobics studio
at the mall

is replaced with a pricey clothes store,
exploding with vivid hues, and I cry
to Cyndi Lauper's "True Colors"
every damn time
because nobody sees my *true colors*.

All they see is
some misfit chick
trying to blend in
stand out
shape up
slim down
and hide that

Lose Weight!
Lose Weight!
Lose Weight!

her life has no direction.

Back to the Future, Part 2

My BC3 English professor
was a pro football player
briefly. He drives a red Porsche
and compares
Shakespeare's "Romeo and Juliette"
to the season his team
got eliminated from the playoffs
during the same round
as their greatest rival.

He is definitely making my writing worse.

After one semester,
I drop out
due to the lack
of a plot.

Daydream Believer

Family and acquaintances
and friends of my mother
say I should model.

"You're so tall." "Photogenic!"
        "All legs and cheekbones."

They throw hollow praises.
I'm not skinny anymore,
but the compliments land.
I want to live the fairy tale,
want to be special,
and modeling
seems the fastest, easiest way.

I've already got a jumpstart
on the eating disorder.

Approached at the mall,
I sign up for classes
at John Casablancas Elite Models.
They train us
to put on makeup
walk in heels
twist our torsos
to look thin-thinner-thinnest in photos

Mom is elated
I'm living out her beautiful dream.

It's Up to You, NY

I yank my roots, quick and hard
from the soft green earth
where they have grown.
Rush from Butler, PA,
to the New York I've longed for.

Mom and Lewis think
it's my ill-fated mission
to save my father,
but I only want
to save myself
from this aimless *not*-New York life.
I load my car with a
black steamer-trunk of
clothes, makeup, and dreams
head east on 80.

I watch God's handiwork yield
to man's inferior attempts
at lasting greatness.
Hours and miles to think
flicking spent cigarettes out the window

I vow
a fresh start all around.

Just need to lose
a few pounds first.

Level Up

I arrive at Lucy's apartment
at two in the morning
knock loud and long until
she groggily answers the door.

On the phone
she seemed psyched to have
her pseudo-little-sister
come crash.
I should have told her
when I was arriving
but threw all my change
into the basket for the GW Bridge
none left for a pay phone.

Lucy is wearing
her boyfriend's shirt
down to her knees
face closed tight
against the hallway light.
"I'm here!"
I announce with a happy flourish.
She mumbles, "You sure are,"
on her way back to bed
I whisper it to myself again,
I'm here.

Imposter 4

I am the worst
waitress ever.
Can barely pronounce
half the specials
forget to bring customers
superfluous items
drinks
side dishes
and forks.
Am always frantically
"in the weeds!"
and dread
each and every table
seated in my section.
Prefer hanging out in the kitchen
with the Spanish-speaking staff who
laugh and smile at me
as I stomp and bark
the joke Lucy taught me,
"No mejora, cabrón!"
delivered with a wide grin.
We are all newly arrived,
starting over,
reckless, wild, and alive.

I love sharing shifts with
Crystal, my age
my height
but thinner
with slim hips that the kitchen guys don't see
commenting instead on my full ones.

She is famous for using
the Heimlich Maneuver to save
a choking customer
who wasn't even seated in her section.

She gets my humor,
thinks I'm quirky "in a good way."
Explains New York to me
while constantly pulling me
out of the weeds.

Adventures in Waitressing

I drop the first lobster I serve,
watch him slide across the floor
riding his deep silver lid
like a sled.
I hide my laughter
privately flip him back onto a plate
stage his claws and antenna
to look natural.

My method of uncorking
expensive bottles of wine
worth more than my car
is downright comical
locking pantyhosed knees
I knot my face
and swear under my breath.

"Out to eat" usually meant
a place with a drive-through window,
never with servers wearing bowties,
and lobster on the menu.
This is not a place
I belong.

But I keep my lipstick fresh
flash an even smile
and make customers laugh
as I beg them to *please*
not order the duck.

Within weeks, I'm promoted to
the Businessman's Tap Room
where I swap out my black
tie and cummerbund
for pink satin.
Trafficking my looks
and affecting a fake
folksy accent,
for bigger tips.
Swallowing bitter guilt
each time I pass
the genuinely good server
who trained me.

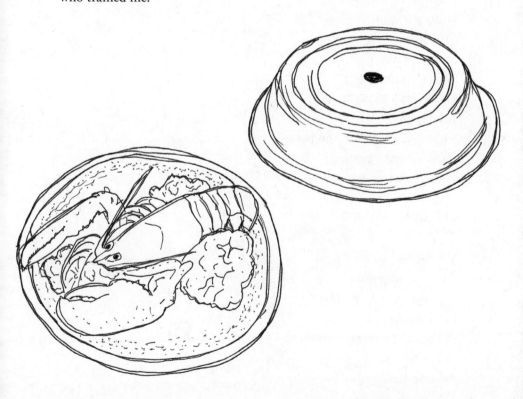

Party Girl

My first night out
at a bar with Lucy
and her boyfriend
we discover
I am *not* a *cool* drunk.
A few fuzzy navels in, I am
pounding my fist proclaiming,
"Just wait until I turn twenty-one!"
I give a loud "Whooo"
as each drink appears until
Lucy's boyfriend
takes me by the shoulders
tells me urgently,
"You need to *dig yourself.*
You are underage.
You are being loud.
People are looking at you.
Just . . . . . *Dig Yourself.*"
I spend the rest of the night
nodding and repeating
to everyone and no one
"I'm digging myself.
I'm digging myself."

On the way home
I spew orange puke
neatly into a paper bag, then
laugh hysterically at the gag
of the bag's missing bottom.

No wonder
Dad loves drinking.

Skirmish

Crystal has an arsenal of
cute friends
I crush on a husky one,
despite her warning
      "He's a dog."
I'm thrilled
he likes me back.

We talk, laugh
go out for drinks at dance clubs
where I dance and he drinks.
After, we make out
in the family room of his house
while his parents sleep,
      presumably—
      I've never met them.
And I perpetually block
his barrage of attempts
to have sex,
      because frankly
      I'm scared of sperm.

He takes me on a weekend trip
to a cabin upstate,
asks if I like champagne
"Not really" I respond
right before he presents
a classy pink bottle.
He pouts at how I've ruined
his perfect surprise

and I give him a
consolation blow job
      because, hey, I barely ate today
      and my sperm-o-phobia
      happens to be
      fertilization specific.

Heist

After our ~~romantic~~ getaway
I notice
my bulky boyfriend
stops asking me questions
about myself
like I'm a mystery
he's lost interest in solving.
His gaze wanders
around the club,
eyes now pausing
on other girls' butts

that always
look better
than your cursed one.

I need him to notice *me*.

I take action,
grab his hand
silently lead him out
to where my car sits benignly
in the parking lot.

I climb into my passenger seat
recline it back as far as it will go,
which is not actually all that far.
Suggestively, I invite him in.
He asks if I'm sure
because "things
are about to get real."
I just want to mess around.
But think of Crystal

hearing I'm a virgin
telling me
the worst thing a girl can be
is a tease.

I nod, ready
for things to get real,
although I'm certain that
I'm not.

But I have his
full focus
more engaged
than ever.
Pupils swollen.
He's all mine.

My smash and grab
for attention
a success.

Steam drapes draw closed
across all the windows.
He positions his thick torso
over me
I panic
Oh wait
"I have my period,"
  whew
I feign deep regret
hope Crystal isn't right.

Fuck Me

His reaction
to my time of the month
is all wrong.
His grin brightens
and he says
this means
I can't get pregnant right now.

I suspect
his intel
is flawed but
it's not like I planned any of this.
I just wanted him to stop looking
at other girls' butts.

I fought for his attention,
and now I have it.

All his hot beer breath on my face.
All his shoving my skirt aside
positioning maxi pad panties askew.
All his thrusting
from above.
I feel him inside me
fleetingly think
This is it
I'm really doing it
I'm having sex.

And yet it does not feel
sexy.
Nothing like
I've imagined.

I try to guard
My midsection.
                              More like MAX-section!
We've never been
fully naked together
                    because damn *that is a lot of bloat!*
This would be a bad time
for him to notice
                                        You have
                        a disgusting amount
                                            of flab.

I don't want
his attention on
                            that fat pigbitch body
                just look at your glowing pale skin
                jiggling by the light of the streetlight
I want to disappear.

But he seems to be enjoying
what is happening
between us
my wired nerves ignored.
Like I'm missing this.

I push away self-loathing
but can't quite find the rhythm
before he's tapping my hip
to signal he's almost done

so I slide out of the way which is
        heh
not an easy maneuver.
Panic
        the sperm are coming!
I'm moving away too slow.

The unmarried seat belt buckle
bites into my ass cheek where my
worst pair of cotton undies
stretch across
like a butt-shash
        my buttocks won
        the pageant after all
my prize is
his jizz
all over my crumpled skirt.

After

Flushed
satisfied
he folds thick arms around me.
I feel
connected.
Definitely
not a mistake.

Except
if I'd known
we'd end up here anyway,
I kinda wish
I'd gone for the
pink-champagne-scenario.

> *Oh, really? Instead of*
> *losing your virginity*
> *in your smelly car*
> *ya fat slut?*

Fuck Me 2

He leans in.
I smile.
He whispers,
"Now you can tell
your friends back home
you moved to New York
and got fucked,"
which is a pretty funny joke
except I ruin it
by starting to cry.

He backpedals,
says he loves me,
is going to drive
to Pennsylvania
meet my parents
"marry the hell" out of me.
I cling to his proposal,
ignore the seatbelt buckle
burrowing a bruise into the *despicable*
butt that got me into this mess.

Fuck Me 3

My ploy to keep my boyfriend
hooked
with the lure of my virginity
is weak.
Like our sex life,
carries no momentum.
My *Cosmopolitan* magazines
have plenty of sex advice,
but for other
sexy confident girls
                      with thinner thighs.

So it's a total shock
yet no surprise when
my first New York boyfriend
breaks up with me a week later.
Knocking the air from my lungs
with *sorry, but at least
I told you in person.*

For days I pace around
Lucy's apartment
waiting for him
to change his mind
hugging my pillow
tight to my stomach,
to keep my insides
from spilling out
ugly cry so hard
half my face is freckled
with broken blood vessels.

I feel cracks forming, unable to catch my breath,
a steady fountain of tears and snot
hyperventilating into hiccups

But hey, at least
you're too upset
to eat.

Home Alone

Lucy shares her
breakup music mixtape
tries to teach me
healing rituals,
    like pouring milk
    directly into the carton of ice cream.
                    Nice try, porky.

Crystal swoops in,
taking my side against the dog-guy
she warned me about.
We have an all-out
Menstruation Celebration
when my late period finally comes.
Flush with most joyous Ka-swoosh!

I set off on a spontanious solo
road trip home
cathartic screamcrysinging
the whole way, ignoring
fellow traveler's stares.

Arrive to find
Lewis sheet-rocked the basement
with the fixed fireplace
moved Christopher down there.
I stay in his old room,
with only one window
and stacks of Marvel comics everywhere.

A gaping dirt hole fills the side yard,
for a new swimming pool

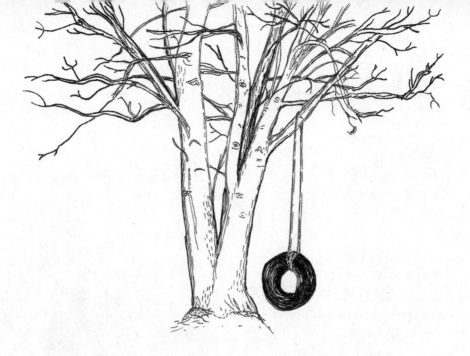

a smooth-walled
square-cornered cavity
with an eight-foot drop to the bottom
so wide and so deep I could drown in it.

The whole house bustles around me.
Cara and Chris in high school
with friends
nobody needs
a ride to soccer.
Wiener dog puppy
accepts my affection but
doesn't know me.
Follows Lewis.

My family renovated
with new hope and fun
a sense of purpose and ease,
but somehow forgot to leave
space for me.

Girls Just Wanna . . .

Back in New York
ready to try again
show everyone
I'll do something
special with my life.

Through with guys,
Crystal and I declare
      GIRL'S!! NIGHT!! WOO!!
Click click click into clubs
in sky-high heels
each of us six feet tall.
Collecting attention
and free drinks.

Some nights we wear
fake diamond rings
feign engagement
to be left alone.
Others, we chase meaningless kisses
skillfully sucking face with the faceless.

"Chicks Before Dicks," our mantra,
I am finally "Super Chick"
as I drink away my suspicion that
deep down
I'm just chasing
that intoxicating
first hit kiss high from Jonathan.

Fuck Me For Real

We are at a house party
thrown by four boys
of varied cuteness
with a gross couch
I plan to sleep on.
Crystal and I have a
never-leave-a-friend-behind
ironclad policy
and she is definitely
spending the night.
I've had too much to drink
—four flat warm beers
on an empty stomach.
More than the stained sofa
I *dread* facing
the four-guy-bathroom situation.

I can't hold it any longer
head into the hall and am hijacked
by a lanky boy
I made out with earlier,
when I was still sober.

A college student
friend of a friend
of the party throwers
who leads me by the hand
takes a hard
left into
the biggest bedroom right
beside the bathroom,

I try to explain I seriously
need to pee.

The dimly lit band posters
trade places as
I'm spun inside
tipped onto
the bed, jeans peeled off
and college boy
forces his fingers inside me
hard.
In a way that does
not feel good
couldn't possibly
be meant to feel good.

I consider acting
grateful
so his finger foreplay
can end but he's so rough
       this is painful
I can't even pretend
watch the shadows on the ceiling
flinch as he kisses my face
try to make it stop
politely because
I don't want to make a big fuss
or a scene or anything,
       maybe he's just
       genuinely terrible at this
I keep repeating I really
really please need to pee
half-laughing

so he won't feel rejected.
I promise to come right back
but he doesn't stop
jamming
     jamming
          jamming his fingers
inside me
my rogue brain wonders
is he also braiding scotch tape
in my hair

suddenly
he stops because the lights flash on
there is a sticky
puddle on
the bed and the owner of the now bloody comforter is screaming and I
run to the bathroom slam the door, huddle in the filthy corner, hands
over my ears as I cry and cry and cry and cry and cry
                            until I'm finally numb.

The Door

Over the sound of my sobs
the yelling gradually stops
Crystal's soft voice
outside the door
tells me to let her in.

I sit on the closed lid of the toilet
we both stare at the floor.
I adjust the toilet paper
stuffed in
the crotch of my jeans. Wince.

"You don't have
your period."
Not a question.
Our cycles are synched.
She knows that isn't
period blood
pooled on the bed.

As she drives us home
my ears ring with
rage that my

stupid body

would splash
across an angry stranger's comforter
humiliating you again.

I force the galvanized image
of my bright blood
in the center of that pale bed
as far down as it will go
clanking into
my basement consciousness
where all my bad experiences
and darkest thoughts fester
and fuse together.

My resolve
a steel door guarding
the entrance to that
dark basement.

It never happened.

Like all the other
exiled memories
this one eventually
gets tired of fighting and
goes to sleep.

Safe Sex

Crystal and I don't discuss
the college boy
or the ~~assault~~ comforter incident
> *because really,*
> *what could we possibly say?*
but remain sex-positive
my post-virginity era
sex is *no big deal* after all
no point
> in saying no
to the *next* guy
> who thinks I'm beautiful.

I insist
on a condom at least.
Fear of sperm
pregnancy and AIDS
finally making me bold.

I try to enjoy myself.
But my
> fat stomach bulges
> wide ass flaps
brain draws focus from the way
my body feels.
> He's going to realize
> you're not beautiful.

At least I'm secure in the fact
that the *next* guy
can't break my heart.
I barely care about him at all.

Good Day

Sugarfree candy,
coffee,
and cigarettes all day.

City of Dreams

We question our
acting teacher's qualifications.
Her credits include
"nothing we've heard of,"
there's no way to
"look her up."
She gives us cheesy dialogue
circa the 1950s
lapses into dramatic asides
without warning.
We are, after all,
a paying audience
laugh at her eccentric outfits,
scarves and beads and
broomstick skirts
likely stolen
from a dusty set.

During a scene
that has me
flirting it up
with a knobby-looking boy
too nervous
to stay in character,
she *stops everything*
announces to the whole class
they should
keep an eye out for me.
Declaring
I have what it takes
to make it
looks   talent   drive

"Mark my words:
remember this face,"
she roughly squeezes my cheeks.
          "You will see this girl again."

And so she is now
the most *brilliant* teacher ever
although she doesn't give
advice or direction.
Plus her monologues mean
we run out of class time
before I can perform
the one I've memorized:
Dirty Dancing.
          Where Baby
          confronts her father
          and apologizes
          for letting him down
          but says he let her down too.
Armed with my mortal mentor's faith,
I hit Manhattan's magical streets
scour the back page of *Backstage*,
for go sees and open calls.
Hungrily hunting for
my breakthrough.
I get signed
at the first agency
I audition and ready myself
to find out just how special I am.

Four / Girl Goes Wild

Wannabe

There are all kinds of shitty showbiz jobs
and I commence combing my way through them.

PC Expo at Javits Center
I tower in heels
handing out
floppy disk startup trade show pamphlets.

Am told they appreciate my enthusiasm
"but *please* stop trying
to explain the software."

A graveyard photo shoot
for a supermarket rag
titled, *True Story*
to run alongside a piece
about a girl's dead dad
she can't forgive.
My green suede skirt
"all wrong"
my reddened eyes
won't stop watering
from the makeup and wind,
which is unfortunate
because the girl in the story
doesn't cry for her dead dad.

Posing
for a catalogue
the photographer rants
about my cuticles as if
they're not attached to a human being

with ears and feelings.
Apparently, manicures
are an unspoken norm,
I've never had one,
can't imagine
paying good money
when I have an ocean of
wet *n* wild polish at home.

A runway star, not at Fashion Week,
modeling wedding gowns for eager brides-to-be.
Not aggressive enough
as a department store perfume sprayer
but find my groove goofing around
with guys at golf outings,
helping the men
laugh and spend money.

Finally, a non-speaking role.
Pretending to talk on the phone.
I way overact,
flipping pale, damaged hair in fake glee.
      Typical ridiculous
     embarrassing talentless clown.

I channel my inner-Sequinette,
wearing elaborate costumes
to gigs with an event DJ.
I am a sexy pirate. Salsa dancer.
Space cadet in knee-high silver boots.
Dance everything
from ballroom to vogue.
Perform at bar mitzvahs,
birthday bashes and holiday parties
all over Manhattan.

At Windows on the World,
        the top floor of One World Trade,
I stand on a speaker,
buzzed from free screwdrivers
teaching party guests
how to pantomine Y and M and C and A
dancing with earnest abandon
I am not too much
look out through
the back wall of windows
constellation of lights
twinkling far below.
This city is mine.

Or it will be.
I want everything.
Lust for NY like a ~~lover~~
jealous girlfriend.

I cannot get enough
just wish I could make
NY love me back.

Possessed

Lucy and her boyfriend are
out at a party,
I am dressed like a cat
handing peanut butter cups to trick-or-treaters,
      my favorite. *The candy, not the brats.*

We overbought and so the witching hour ends
with an orange plastic pumpkin head
still filled with orange squares.

I have not eaten all day
imagine
I deserve
just one.

        You are wrong.
          You are weak.

I eat
them all.

Peanut butter
      my old arch-nemesis.
        You are a wretched,
          wretched girl.

Tricked by
      Treats.

The Beginning

Whispers of damnation
swirl in my head.
I am nauseous with disgust,

> Hey, now
> there's an idea.

Approach the toilet.   Lift the lid.

Apply pressure to stomach
swollen under black micro-skirt.
Kneel on the cold floor.
Fishnets bite my kneecaps
desperation claws my throat.
I steady my breath
slide my thighs open
straddle the bowl.

> That's right you whore
> into position
> Get this fucking filth   out
> Now now now   before you get
> fat fat fat.

Turn the clock back about one-half hour.
Limbo under the descending bar of my dignity.

Bitter/Sweet Victory

Long middle finger
in my mouth
the way I imagine it is done
by those bulimics in Mom's old class notes.

Breathing through my nose,
this seems silly,
but then. I feel the thick sweet mass
pushing up and out
splashing into the bowl,
cold toilet water sneezing in my face.

The blob floats slowly down
to the mouth at the other end and
    I am   *saved*.

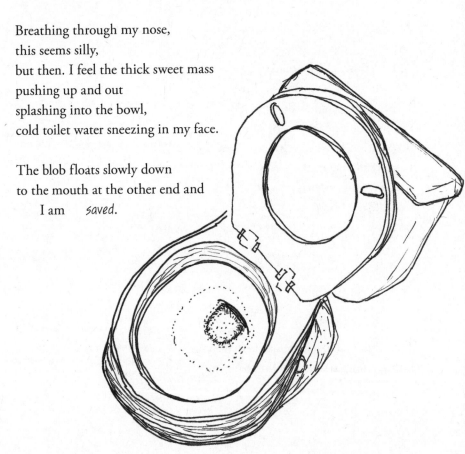

Joystick

I could cry with relief.
Wash my hands,
look at my reflection
see I am crying after all.

Moonlit-rose cheeks are streaked
with smoky-black shadow.
I look deep in my eyes
see something
I don't recognize,
something   off.

You're fine
did good.

I'm numb and a little thirsty but
definitely

back in control.

The Vow

I promise myself it was
just-this-once.

But the next time I
find myself
with a fat bellyful of regret,
I know just what to do with it.

In the Zone

I turn Pro
    the whistle blasts

                            penalty called for
                     excessive mac-n-cheese

    magic time
wide rocking stance
    concentrating
facing down my own basket
    focus
She shoots
    perfect aim!
Nothin' but porcelain
    extremely FOUL SHOT.

Aftergame Dance

The ultimate buzz-kill
comes in a wave

follows the relief
ruining my high

carrying me to the mirror.
I look into addict eyes

whisper *never again*
every time.

                                                        Liar.

Septic Abuse

The toilet breaks
     must be replaced
our landlady
     who exclusively wears
     pastel housecoats
     even with snow boots
is pissed,
        but I find it
    kind of hilarious
        and Lucy claims
   it's a solid excuse
   to be late on rent.

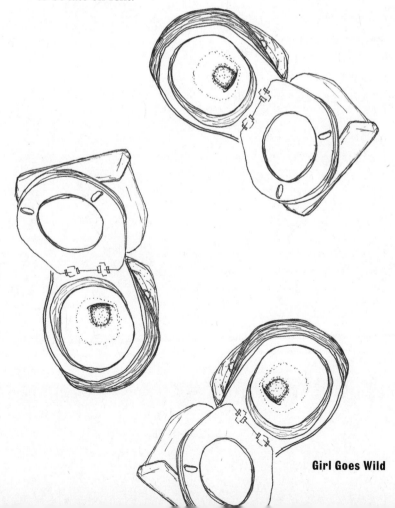

Family Reunion

My dad comes by
he doesn't look so good.
His lifestyle has swollen his belly
shriveled his legs
yellowed his hair.

I don't look so good
gaunt and glassy-eyed
my nose won't stop running.

He blames cocaine. *Nope.*
bad girls do drugs,
nice girls like me
just get eating disorders,
but I let him think
I'm a cokehead.
It's less embarrassing, besides

my life
has nothing to do with him.

Three's Company

Lucy's having a baby.
Her hormones and my moods
a combustible cocktail, mixing up
blasting emotions
and shouting matches.

Mid-fight over yet another
forgotten dirty cereal bowl,
     —mine—
I walk away,
splash water on my face
at the bathroom sink
give Lucy time to realize
she's overreacting but she
smashes through the bathroom door
with renewed rage
while I'm drying
my face on a towel.
A towel currently hanging
on the back
of that bathroom door.

I see a flash,
howl
as blood
drips
and Lucy
immediately drops down
to catch me
so fiercely sorry.

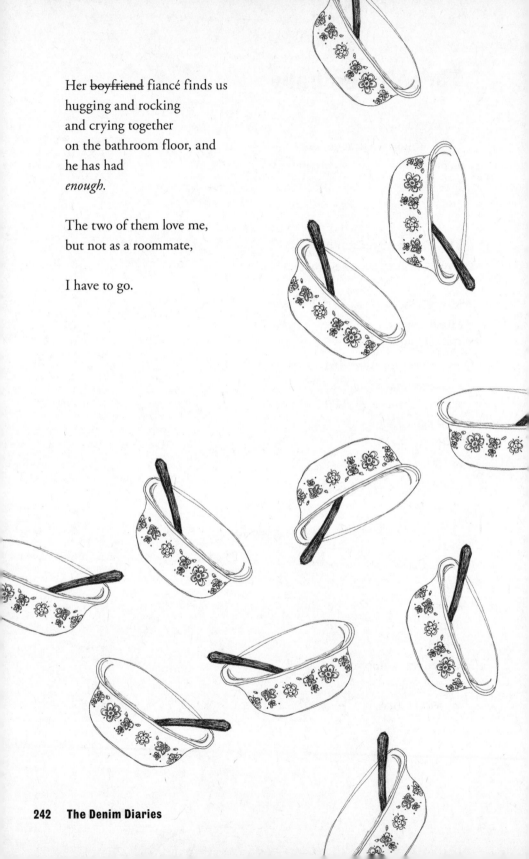

Her ~~boyfriend~~ fiancé finds us
hugging and rocking
and crying together
on the bathroom floor, and
he has had
enough.

The two of them love me,
but not as a roommate,

I have to go.

Love Shack

I move to Levittown, Long Island
with Crystal and friends.
We are: four girls, each uniquely pretty
and four guys, all named Mike.
A mostly platonic arrangement
considering the people involved.

We are artists and musicians
working blue-collar jobs
rather than wasting time at college
besides Crystal
who graduated early.

Festering piles of bored potential.
60s communal living
reenacted in the late 80s,
with lots of heavy metal long hair
and a scuffed drum kit
where a kitchen table belongs.

Peace and love and
bitchy confrontations,
like a reality show
except the only ones watching us
are the neighbors and they are not fans.

Quick to judge
quicker to call the cops
when we get a little loud.

But the police know
we are only

trying to have a little fun.
Ask that we please,
have the live band
playing Van Halen
"sign off by ten."
and, "Maybe keep
the *occupancy* down."

Mother Crystal

We each "have issues'"
      as mom would say
some party too much
some cheat on their girlfriends
      and mysteriously awake
      to slashed tires.
some are morose
      boiling bird skulls
      for gruesome gothic art.
One girl just had yet another abortion
with her ~~boyfriend~~
married boss.
      We shower her with condoms
      not judgement.

One girl with daddy issues
feels everything too much,
chain-smokes constantly,
and flat-out loathes
every inch of her body
      that would be me.

Then there is Crystal,
my stunning auburn friend.
The dominant matriarch,
gifted at drawing,
whose greatest talent
is connecting people
creating togetherness.

She assumes I'm classy
when she hears running water

to cover the sound
when I ~~puke~~ pee.
She can't know,
would make me
stop immediately   *make you fat.*

She's impressed
how much I read
always with an open
mystery novel
or magazine.
Crystal decides
I should take modeling
more seriously.
I've got potential
and she is great at
curating people.

Girlie-Girl Power

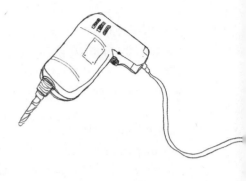

Crystal and I bring out each other's
feisty independence
and creativity as we renovate
our basement space together.

We wield power tools,
lay remnant carpet
spackle designs to mask
crumbling drywall and uneven seams.

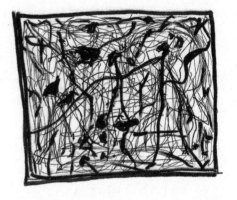

Laughing,
we splatter paint
with abandon that would cause
Jackson Pollock to die again.

We pick out cute boys in bars
like candy,
but never give out our number,
just collect theirs,
stuff matchbooks
and colored slips
of uneven paper into
our 'guy jar' fishbowl.

Crystal decides
we should smoke less.
Resolves
we will start SlimFast.
Teaches me
to never put my purse
on the aisle-side of the train
to always

be aware of my surroundings
to carry mace just in case.
Better to have it and not need it
than need it and not have it.

Crystal reorganizes
my modeling book
shows it to a photographer friend
who suggests I cut my hair to stand out
but *no way!* short hair would only make
my ass look bigger.

Crystal edits and deletes
my wardrobe
makes me a bit less
white-trash-in-the-city.

Insists I lose my
favorite white fringe boots
splurge
on Levis that fit.
Informs me that
"Wearing black is always best."

Clueless
I never realized
how much work I needed
before Crystal
started remodeling me.

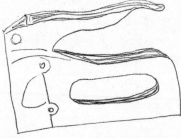

M-m-m-my Tiara

Gliding through the club,
cheekbones aimed high
short skirt revealing
long long legs.
I survey the competition,
am I thinnest of all?

I'm definitely a semi-finalist.

Spot a guy
elbow his inattentive buddy
give a cat-like
nod of approval for his good deed.
That's right, don't miss this vision,
the title is mine.

If I can just stay
in this good lighting,
in my leg-amplifying heels,
I might be
fairest for a moment.
Try to ignore
other rooms,
other pageants, where
other contestants loom
clawing for my fleeting crown.

60s Flashback

Our house is *the* place to hang
a constant flow
of upbeat and/or high friends.
All are welcome.
Crystal's grey bunny
freely shits everywhere,
I walk around with a parakeet on the shoulder
of my floor-length peacock robe. Our lease says no dogs or cats.
Upstairs, thick pot plants grow
      Stoner-Mike's shockingly elaborate private garden,
      built with tinfoil and sunlamps
      in a rare flurry of activity and ingenuity.
Our ancient, dresser-sized television
claims one corner of the living room
playing a bootleg copy of Woodstock
on a loop.
      Three days of music, peace, and love
      reminiscent of
      long-ago Jesus festivals.

Our whole house worships Woodstock.
Sure, we Want Our MTV, with its
24/7 all music videos all the time,
I, personally,
wouldn't want to live in a world
without Blockbuster video rentals
but Crystal instigates
our collective lament that
we are all twenty years too late
to experience the once-in-a-lifetime event
of Woodstock.

This is your brain.

this is drugs.

this is your brain on drugs.

One clear Saturday,
Crystal wakes me with
get dressed quick, we're
heading north in her blue hatchback
backwards in time
on a holy pilgrimage.

Two hours later, we've asked
four separate strangers
for Yasger's farm,
discover 'Woodstock'
happened an hour and a half
outside Woodstock.
Two more hours of
wrong turns
and blank looks
before we hunt down the spot,
step out of the car

stare with reverence
across the vast field
picturing the stage
and that life-changing event.

We ache for it.

The gruff strains
of Joe Cocker singing
*With a Little Help
From My Friends*
stream from the car and cling
to the honeysuckle air like an apparition.
We squeal and hug, jump and

dance through the grass.
Crystal is beyond ecstatic
        to be here-right-here-really-here,
and I'm caught up
in her unbridled elation
and also
truly thrilled
to be out of the car.

Retched Removal

In the basement rec room
where our bedrooms connect,
amidst 60s beaded curtains,
stained glass lamps,
macramé pillows, gathered
from yard sales, curbsides,
and our favorite-Mike's mom,
we talk
late into the night,
frank discussions about
sexuality, racism, addiction,
abortion, religion and
spirituality, which we both agree
is a separate thing from religion.

We are both *spiritual*.
But I won't let her
use her tarot cards on me,
> *not because*
> *I don't believe*
> *they have power*
> *but because*
> *I'm quite certain they do.*
She respects my confession that
despite my current lack of churchgoing
> *Jesus remains*
> *in my life.*
> *Still lives in my heart.*
We challenge each other
share experiences
hopes and dreams
> *literally*
> we endlessly dissect our dreams

our minds connect and swing
open
both free
to lay everything bare.

Except
I can never quite bring myself
to come clean
about my food thing.

With eight people
two toilets
and no bathroom in our
underground space,
I rarely have
privacy for purging.
Start using
the blue plastic trashcan
in my bedroom to hold
night deposits.

Crystal is gone early each morning,
working her way up
at some fancy city office
toward a solid future,
while I sleep past noon
in a room with no windows,
        a trace scent of vomit
and a life with few responsibilities,

        aside from taking out
        the disgusting trash.

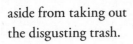

Phone Home

Mom mails me a fat envelope of
family photos and
Christopher has gotten tall
a cool, asymmetrical haircut
over one eye.
I smile until I flip
to Cara.
I knew they
were busy building
a huge addition to
our hopeful house
but didn't know Cara
had renovated into
a breathtakingly beautiful   *and thin*
blue-eyed goddess.

I don't recognize the teen
posing playfully,
kicking one toe in the air.
> *wasn't she supposed to have*
> *an awkward phase*
> *in there someplace?*
It wasn't enough for her to be
"the smart one,"
now she gets to be
"the pretty one" too?

Home suddenly feels distant
in a different way.

Fuck Me 4

I go on a date
with a hot guy whose sick car
makes all the Mikes swoon.

As he drives
he slides a hand to my thigh
claims it's not fair
my perfect legs have such an effect on him.
I smile shyly and reposition them
to look thinner.

The two of us turn
every head as we enter the club,
The Cure
infuses the air with longing.
We are strikingly beautiful
together. But must exit early and fast
when he spots his "crazy" ex.

Back in my bedroom,
he shows me his
tattoo,
the image of Animal drumming
on his otherwise flawless butt cheek.
"Yup," I say,
"that's a Muppet on your ass alright."

I make out with him anyway,
things escalate quickly, but
I am clear.
I don't want sex tonight.

He laughs.
Eases me back on my bed.
Pulls a condom
from his back pocket
a teasing smile
on his handsome face
> *So smug.*
> *So certain*

rolls on the rubber,
and coaxes
my perfect legs apart. I
lie rigid, detached,
my thighs wide my
insides dry my
mind
trying to calculate
whether I'm allowed
to feel violated.
> *I was into him*
> *before introductions to*
> *the ex and Animal.*
I taste copper outrage
that I decide to swallow down
along with the urge
to wail on him like the
drumming star of his pumping buttocks.

> *Ahhhhhh! Ahhhhhh! AHHHHHH!*

At least
he's lightning-quick.

The next morning
when I emerge from my room
Crystal asks
how my date went,
and since the hot guy
with the sick car
and the Muppet butt
is still asleep in my bed
I answer honestly,
"Still happening."

Paying Dues

The modeling world has a sleazy underbelly
only wannabes like me get to see.
Many traps designed to snare
      country-mouse-girls
         trying to make it in Manhattan.

Alone at a studio,
a photographer explains as if to a child
that if I have sex with him,
we will have better chemistry
when he shoots off
his roll
      of film.

Promises he can get me the jobs
and exposure I crave,
moves in close
kisses me as
I stand hugging myself.
He tastes old
my dad's age
don't want to even picture his junk
      let alone see it
         let alone touch it
my daddy issues become sentient
      and recoil
         pulling me backward.
At last, a limit to my self-loathing

And I'm all out of consolation blow jobs.

I grab
the gullible outfit changes I've brought,
shaking with revulsion,
or fear
        or perhaps low blood-sugar,
I flee.
            I'd hoped this was my
            big break.
            Not just another snake.

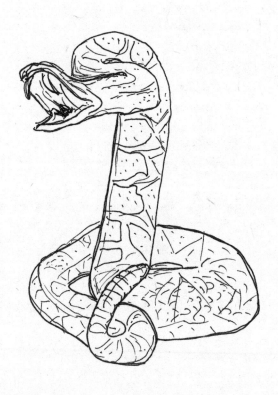

Prayer Request

A talent scout
comes to evaluate
the agency's most promising models
one-on-one
me included.

Clutching my portfolio
I assess the chosen few,
each of us smiling insincerely with gauging eyes.
I am intimidated by my thin rivals
but silently will the universe

Pick me. Pick me. Pick me.

My Big Break

She glances brusquely
through my portfolio
says I photograph *beautifully*
leans close,
looks into my eyes
and calls me FAT.

Sure, she sugarcoats it,
explains how THIN models need to be.
Blames those TEN camera pounds.
Says to lose, say, TWENTY and
gives me her phone number.

My heart beats in my red face
as I nod with enthusiasm.
Of course you are right,
what was I thinking,
sorry for wasting your time.
This prick stings worse
than being propositioned.
I grab my gullible Look Book
and flee.

Nearsighted

Lifeless.
My teeth tingling
   they hurt a lot lately
from the task of crunching
a whole bag of Doritos,
   tangy triangles of comfort.
The sharp taste
stale on my tongue.

I pull a worn subway token
from my tight pocket
look down at fingers
branded by
shameful orange nacho dust.

That agent lady may be
a Big Shot talent scout. Know
the business. Understand
modeling.
But she wouldn't recognize
a young girl's dreams
if she stepped all over them.

The Quest

I find a public restroom
the scent
so powerful
it must be
on purpose somehow,
like those bakeries
that pump sugary air
to attract customers,
urine-scented ammonia
to advertise a piss station.

The air
invading my nostrils
makes my job easier.
After
my pilgrimage to the glass.
I lean over a sink of ashes
gaze through a blur of tears
into wide brown eyes.

I lock onto my reflection.
Stand entranced as
                    bile

        delicately
        drips

        from my
        fingertips.

I stare deeper
into my
watery eyes,
red from my retching
bringing out the green,
they are
empty.

Where'd I go?

                              stop searching.
                                  give up.
                            What made you
                              ever think
                  you could be special anyway?

The Meet Cute

I constantly threaten to pick
a random name from the "guy jar"
but never do.
The promise of free food and drinks loses
to hanging with Crystal and company
again and again,
and after all
there is no such thing as free.

We go out to a dive bar
that doesn't card.
As I raise my lighter
to one of my slims,
a deep voice
behind my ear says,
"You can't smoke here."

Annoyed, I gesture
to the lightning bug field of lit cigarettes
turn into
a grinning face, handsome features
beauty mark on forehead
as if drawn on by a
Sharpie saying
this one might be
The One.

My Crush

A NYC undercover cop,
twenty-something, long hair,
"like *21 Jump Street*,"
he says with a smirk
laughs at my breaking the law
underage by a year.

Mr. Undercover is street smart
starts most conversations
"Not for nothin' . . ."
One day at his apartment,
he shows off his "buddies,"
Smith and Wesson,
      asks if I want to hold his pistol
      like I'm supposed to be impressed
      so I pretend to be,
            although it's mild compared to the rifle
            I learned to shoot in safety ed class back home.
            That gun knocked me two steps backward
            with its violent kick against my shoulder,
                  like it had a mind of its own.
My Undercover Boyfriend
loves the Ramones
the licorice zing of Sambuca shots
and soon, reportedly, me.
He tells wild stories
about being on the job
vibrates with constant intensity
and makes me feel like I'm the romantic interest
on a cop show.

Red Light-Green Light

Green Light Food List
all is well, life is good
I may move on

-but-

one angry Red bite
and Simon Says

>   STOP what you're doing
>   break into a binge

followed by

>   you guessed it
>   a bow to the bowl.

Reset. Do over. Go back to start.
Red or Green
Bad or Good
to puke or not to puke,
that is the question.

Day-Tripper

Supermarket nirvana.
Bliss washes over
as automatic doors swing wide.

Expertly
I gather the perfect combination
of salty sweet salty
sweet salty sweet,
  with a dash
  of red dye #3 and yellow dye #5.
  . . . oh how I love
  food that is orange.

The cheaper the better;
generic is best.

Creme cookies - 99 cents
Sour cream and onion chips - 79 cents

Store brand ice cream - buck-fifty
Day-old donuts
and cheez-puffs on sale

How-to Bulimia
on $10 a day or less.

My Hitchcock Moment

Mr. Undercover interrupts my pork-out,
pulling in the driveway
to surprise me, it works,
        my heart starts thumping
        inside my ears.

My mind hums with alarm
I'm in an underwater dream
willing my limbs
to move faster than time
half-eaten bags of chips
and cookies
quickly jammed into
the old black dreamer steamer trunk
that dominates
a corner of my room.

In slow motion
I stuff one final
empty ice cream carton
toss the spoon,
watch as it
leisurely ~twists~ in the air
taking its time
a clumsy baton trick
tripping me up
getting me *caught*
SLAM the lid shut just-in-time.

Pretend to be thrilled
our bellies bump as we hug hello.

Mr. Undercover laughs
chats about dinner plans,
while I silently will him
to stay the *fuck* away from that trunk.

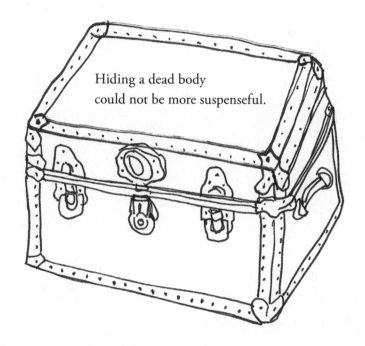

Hiding a dead body
could not be more suspenseful.

Nearsighted 2

I love my Mr. Undercover,
but count on him being a lousy detective.
Until he confronts me
with soft concern.

Holds a mirror to my face,
points out my gauntness,
dark circles under my eyes.
His buttinski-stupid-sister
explained bulimia to him.

I promise to stop. We share
an Oprah-worthy moment.
Audience says, *Awwww,*
we cry and embrace
all while I'm
watching for a commercial break
to get some alone time
with a frigging toilet.

She's a Witch

I'm more careful
exercising my craft.
Go casually to the bathroom after each meal.
Run the water, do my business
brush my teeth,
the smell of my breath a constant concern,
wipe away every damning droplet of evidence,
heartbeat chasing my actions.

Mr. Undercover is amazing, but
     Not for nothin' . . .
I can't handle the steady dread
of getting busted.

Unreliable Narrator 2

Our three-month romance
is less *tunnel of love,*
more *roller coaster,*
filled with heart-pounding climbs
        as sex becomes sex, sex, SEX,
gut-punching downhill drops
        his fidelity seems suspect.
But I'm strapped in for the thrill,
still think he's The One.
        Crabs can come from public toilets, right?

He's truly good to me
except maybe
        that one time he
        held me up against the wall
        by my neck
        in a jealous rage
        over a guy friend
        who calls everyone,
        "Honey."

He was *so sorry* after.
How can I be upset,
when he just loves me *so hard.*

Except now Mr. Undercover
is investigating me
watching my eating
too closely,
time for me to be strong,
        Love is a Battlefield!

I rise up
kick him out of my life,
protect my secrets
so much better
than I ever did my self-respect.

Alone at last
I climb back aboard
my *merry-go-round* relationship
       The truly dysfunctional one
       I have
       with food.

Nightcrawler

Visiting home after the breakup
I consume every last morsel on my plate.
Mother forever monitoring
my "eating thing,"
she doesn't know
my clever purge loophole.
Clearing the table,
I discreetly dispose of leftovers
with my mouth.

After everyone goes to bed
I continue to eat.
Raid cupboards.
Avoidimg squeaky spots
on the new wood floor.
No sounds
as I stuff my face.

Paranoid of being caught,
I go for a walk in the inky midnight
make myself throw up in our field.
Here in the country
the stars shine
so much brighter,
I see the moon of my youth,
listen to the creek flowing
crickets pulsing, a choir of frogs
whose ancestors I chased

and know that what I'm doing
is fucked up.

The Beginning 2

A new voice comes.
You don't have to do this, it says,

and because I have assumed now for so long
that I have no choice but to do exactly this,

I pause.
Wonder if the new voice could be right.

Step Nine

Dad calls with the
fan-freaking-tastic Newsflash
he has stopped drinking,
          I've heard this before
for good.
          Isn't it always?
we should celebrate!

Dad thinks sober chips
and "sorrys"
can buy time lost
all will go back
as if nothing ever happened,
as if we never broke.
But those kids he left
are older now
          with calloused hearts
          he tries to soften
          with his old trick
          humor.
I am not amused.

Divorce changes
more than the present,
it changes the past too.
That old portrait,
blue background
the five of us
huddled together
smiling at the command
of the photographer's

snap snap snap.
Lying through our teeth
to the camera.

Posing as a beautiful family.
That photo
        revealed as counterfeit and
                shoved
                face down
                in a drawer somewhere.

Daddy's Girl 2

Dad and I get together for coffee,
and I admit he seems Different
more present, more solid.

In the car,
I look over
at the thin white scar
dividing his eyebrow
the crack in his façade.
Tell him,
"I don't need a father so much anymore."

I pretend to stare
at my scuffed black boots on the dash
as he drives me home in silence. *There,*

now he hurts too.

Shrinky Dink

Crystal drops by my room
just as I'm about to empty out
      evacuation efforts delayed.

Her eyes meet
my distended belly
as we talk about
"cute Mike,"
the one she made out with once
who is growing increasingly
obsessed with her.
Crystal warns
I should maybe watch my diet.
      What a Control FREAK.

I rush upstairs,
set about the efforts
I intended all along.
Shower and dress
in a tight black tank top with jeans.
      Showing off my expert crisis response.

Crystal laughs
when I come downstairs.
Says those sweats
must have just made me
      look fat.

Runner Up 3

My shining star little sister
takes a field trip
to my New York commune
and we frolic through the city.
I'm the seasoned guide
showing off my Manhattan
she's the wide-eyed tourist.

We get lost
on the subway
three times.

A handful of baseball players
hit on us, we flirt back
share one of their beers.
One asks Cara if she's a model.
She says no,
but points to me and says I am.
He gives a wry up-and-down
says, "What? A hand model?"

     The.   Flirting.   Halts.

His friend punches his arm,
"Come on, man,
she's pretty."
But Cara and I detest them
for insulting me,
for comparing us, and especially,
for implying jealousy
between sisters.

Grown Ups

Cara's visit
is filled with laughter.
Singing goofy pop songs,
loudly and out of tune
and with all our hearts.
We relive our walks
to a nearby 7-Eleven, Cara confesses
she envied the way
Christopher and I
made up stories together.
Imaginative ideas,
effortlessly flowing.

I admit their closeness in age
made me feel outside,
stuck playing lookout
as they scooped handfuls of quarters
from the mall fountain
money to buy
an army of Smurf figurines.

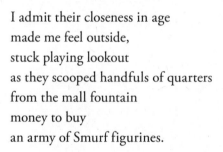

We lounge in the basement sanctum
comparing notes on our "childhood."
bonding over smelly lunch thermoses
filled with milk
and Mom's homemade
brown bread sandwiches
that no one would trade.
We discuss Cara's
college scholarships,
and the novel I'm ~~writing~~
talking about writing.

Together we mourn our Noah's Ark
of dead pets.

Lying
side-by-side
contemplating
my Pollock-esque ceiling,
I'm reminded of
our couch fort oasis
she and Christopher and I
snuggling shoeless
watching TV shows
too young for me.

We scarf cheeze doodles,
ice cream,
and *Mannequin*.
    Epic love between
    muse and artist
    can happen, right?
Cara falls asleep
I watch her,
torn.
    My gut churns.

    You seriously keeping that?
I sneak into the other room

sweaty palms gripping
small blue trashcan.
Utterly desperate.

When my sister starts
her journey home,
I'm struck by the way
she's rearranged everything
in my life
to seem like
a swimming pool-sized
empty hole.

Stormy Sky

Here I stand
on that way high dive
so afraid
so alone
so embarrassed
so exposed.

The water's churning blackness
and I'm just too numb to move

here I wait
wrapped in shame.
No one can help me.
I've been stranded too long.
I know
I'm never getting down.

Atari Break Out

Newly minted mother Lucy
confronts me
about how easily I'm bruising lately.
She scowls with concern that makes me squirm
      and I say "I've gotta go."

My still-sober father
tells me I worry him
he's stuck on the theory I'm doing cocaine
never once tried blow, pretty sure I'd fall for it.
He says let him know if I want help
      I say "I've gotta go."

My dear mother
starts every damn phone conversation
with "How's your eating?"
I cringe and want to hang up.
      "Mom, I gotta go."

Even Crystal
is up my butt
to do *something* about my showbiz career,
"Do you really want to be stuck
waiting tables forever?
You're kind of bad at it."
      "Sorry, but I'm outta here."

Why is every frigging person in my life
such a pain in my wide ass all of a sudden?
Only problem is:
      I'm running out of places to go.

Red Flag

With wonder I study
the results of my purges
creamy clumps and clouds of color,
my latest bold!! new!! creation!!

The tainted taste of acid
resting under my tongue, I ride
the buzz from my retching,
mesmerized as I contemplate
the design I've spent hours fashioning
and bringing forth.
A masterpiece formed in me,
intended for my eyes alone.

I must make sure it is all out
before flushing it away,
what goes in must be released and reviewed.

And now, mixed in with my artwork,
I start to discover swirls
of my own blood.

No Trespassing

I have a secret bigger than life.
People would never believe
my capacity to eat.
The impending doom
of them finding out *looms*.

It is all I think about,
yet something I cannot share.
So no one can know me really
because they cannot know
the biggest part of me.

That secret part.

The part that eats.

Shit Literally Happens

I creep to the bathroom,
the one upstairs
so Crystal and the gang
sharing beers in the kitchen
won't hear.
I have to go,
but just ate a McDonalds happy meal
and guzzled two Bud Lights

> this is the opposite of
> happy and light

Lifting the seat,
I get down on my knees
gag reflex engaged,

> Get those
> sweaty empty calories out NOW.

stomach tensing,
it knows the routine.

> Expunge the gluttony.

With a cramp I remember
ten squares of waxy chocolate
taken earlier, just to be sure
the miserable happy meal wouldn't stick.
Come on, Laxatives,
give a girl a break.

Too late to hold back
contractions and
Fuckballs   Fuck
my trusty Jordache jeans
fill with heat.

And, Scene

Black swirls swim at the edges of my sight.

I have to lie down
just for a minute
rug's wet.
Damn that Stoner-Mike,

why can he never dry
off in the shower
like Crystal always nags?
I'll just rest my head
a quick second, then clean up.

White tile lined with black mildew burns in my eyes.
My mind   separates   surveying the
damage.

not my best performance   what am I doing
about to pass out   on a damp bathroom rug

I silently beg moldy tiles for help
watch the bleak scene fade to black.

Five / Guzzler Girl

The Discovery Channel

One of the Mikes reports dully
"There's a corpse in the bathroom."
All join in carrying me,
banging my head
thump
        thump
                thump
                        down the steps
to my cellar mattress on the floor.

Touch Me

Crystal yells in my ear
pulls my hair, holds my face over
my blue trashcan
encouraging me
       in unwitting parody
to puke into it.

Suddenly lucid
I reanimate
flailing protest.
Crystal shoves my head
      with disgust.
"It's okay. She's alive."

They murmur relief.
Shuffle away.
Leave me alone, confused,
      wanting to die,
drifting back
into the void.

Rise and Shine

Four AM
awake from the dead

can't remember shit
try to figure out how

I got into bed
where

are my pajamas?

What is cold and crumbly inside my jeans
a perfect mold of my butt cheeks?

Damn what's that stench?
    Oh God.
I remember.

Bag My Face

Shame and mortification
do not wash off
in the sea-green bathtub.
        My body
        still finding creative new ways
        to humiliate me.

I dodge my housemates.
They glance at each other
avert their eyes,
avoid me.

Telephoto Lens

They're whispering
what a *headcase*
the small-town girl
turned out to be.
I anxiously wait
for some verdict.

My façade   sha-redded.
I knew I couldn't keep
that sassy super chick act up.
Crystal sits me down
tells me I need to straighten up.
Stop my three C's diet:
          candy, coffee, cigarettes.

"And maybe give up
on the modeling thing.
It's making you weird about food."

Trees of the Field

Alone in the living room
smoking a slim I don't remember
lighting, kneeling
on the worn sofa
just acquired from the curb.
A burnt orange couch carrying
some other family's fort memories.

Outside the picture window
the warm day fades, a large maple
balances itself
inside a narrow strip of earth
bound by sidewalk and curb.
The tree moves
an odd way.
Unnatural
clapping its leaves at me,
reminding me of
a song I used to love.

And all the trees of the field
shall clap their hands.
           clap *clap*

Humming and snapping
I am caught up in lightness

What are you
so fucking joyful about?

the darkening glass
gradually morphs into a mirror

Did you honestly think that tree
was clapping for you?

interrupting me
with my own reflection.

You stupid
embarrassing pigbitch.

Because It Is Bitter

No moon
only yellowed beams
from feeble streetlights.
My back sinks into burnt-orange cushions.
Black thoughts swim and my body
seems far   far   away.

In the distance
my heart
labors to beat.
thump
        thump
I know this is how it ends
for girls like me
who starve, binge, purge.
Desperate bodies feed on hearts.
I tell mine to slow down
thump
            thump
so faint and weak
I could cause it to stop by will.
Shallow breaths, even slower.
At my command it
thump

            thump,
almost stops,
thump

        thump.

Wait!! I don't mean to DIE!

Spirit in the Sky

At the top of the high dive
feeling that old fear.
My knees lock
nowhere to turn
standing above
that black sea of void
reflecting the insatiable
pool of emptiness inside me.

I need

"help."

It's okay, I hear, *I'm here and I've got you.*
I've been here all along.
And there is no strength in me,
only gracemercylove
as I surrender,
and step
into waiting arms.

Confessional

Sobbing
at sticky kitchen counter,
I reach for the notepad
beside the thick answering machine.
Scrounging through drawers
filled with junk,
I find a pen that coughs and
struggles to put forth ink,
words dive onto paper
as if my life depends on it:

You are totally destroying your body.
Starving your brain!
No one can see how SICK you are.
You are sitting here shaking
Have not eaten in days.
You are smart enough to realize
You are acting STUPID
It is time
to stop killing yourself

It is time for you to change.

My housemates come home late
from a party to find
me kneeling in the living room,
the zealous preacher on TV
talking about
salt and light and *hope!*
I ignore their whispers,
continue nodding,
one arm raised in the air
answering, "Amen!"

Crystal pats my head,
tells me I missed one hell
of a night.
I laugh but don't say
I could say the same.

Alternative Lifestyle

With the morning sun
I call my new-improved
zero-percent-alcohol father
reinstate his Dad license.

Thrilled, he decides
I should live with him
despite Crystal's protest
I'm being silly
risking everything
should stay
at the fun house.

She gets home from work
as we are about to pull away
in a borrowed van,
my reloaded, black
steamer trunk in back.

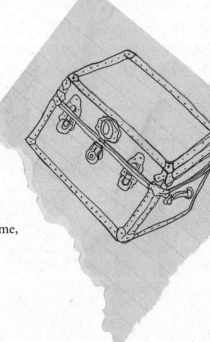

I owe Crystal so much,
love her so much, she
who saw something special in me,
who helped me
become a New Yorker,
taught me style is a mindset,
convinced me I'm cool,
and that guys acting shitty
doesn't mean we deserve it.

We wallow
we cry
we gossip
we laugh
and then
we fix our hair and move on.
She's helped me
believe
I'm strong enough to start over

even without her support.

I hop out,
tackle hug Crystal.
Tell her, "I have to figure
some stuff out, want to
give my dad
a second chance.
We both need this."

She looks me in the eye
both of us with so much still left to say
too much.

Silence stretches between us.

I turn,
crawl back beside my dad
call, "Take good care of the Guy Jar!"
With a smirk and a head shake
she is gone.

Whistleblower 2

One at a time
I tell on myself
to those who care
the biggest pains in my ass
who hurt when they hear.

They meet my dark, writhing words
with love.
Lucy shares her
own struggles.
We form a new challenge
to get well.
And the overwhelming fear
of them all finding out   evaporates.

Flashback

I am five
at a campsite, listening
to the park ranger rant
about dangerous bears in the area
clutching my stuffed Smokey.
Dad scoffs as
the ranger lists the strict rules:
- Hang coolers from trees.
- No snacks in tents.
- Never leave
       dirty dishes
       garbage
       soap
       anything that smells remotely like food
where it might attract bears,
       the bears,
             those goddamn bears.
The zealous ranger
adjusts his green hat, shouts:
       Do *not* feed the bears.
       Do not *feed* the bears.
       Do not feed the *bears*.
He pauses
wiping sweat from red face
asks for questions.
Dad whispers in my ear.
I raise my five-year-old hand
fingers waggling and ask,
"When do we get to feed the bears?"

Dad & Girl

My father and I are great roommates,
stay up late
watching *Seinfeld*, *SNL*, and *Letterman*.
All our cereal bowls are dirty.
We just rinse as we go.
No need to *stress*.

One day strange sounds
come from the living room.
I round the corner to find Dad
sitting on the couch
with a squirming kitten *for me*
ribbon tied clumsily
round itty neck.
My shrieks of glee
send bitty legs pumping.

AA Dad introduces
his merry band of recovery friends
with slogans and optimism and rueful honesty,
the funniest drinking stories . . .

. . . and the most devastating. Lives and loves and
families lost to addiction
powerful regret punching
through the slim veneer
of happiness.

Relapse
waiting around every corner
like a wild bear.

Back to the Future, Part 3

I toss my stacks
of sleek, starry-eyed photos.
Enroll part-time
at Nassau Community College
and join the church that helps Dad stay sober.

I can do this
all that willpower will
crush this eating disorder.
Time to draw on my potential.

And hope.

Apologies to Emily Dickenson, but
my hope does not have feathers. My hope
has claws and fur and teeth
and fills me with
the determination to fight.

Volume Control 2

An experiment.
Make all foods permissible,
eat without restrictions,
grow the Green Light Food List.

I attempt to trust my appetite.
Craving peanut butter cups? I eat 'em.
As many as I want,
which is a LOT
before it sinks in,
I don't have to consume them all now;
legalizing Reese's removes their power.

I crave crunch
and green and fiber. *With protein perhaps?*
Um, salad . . . maybe with shrimp? *Fuck yes!*
and a Reese's chaser if I'm still feeling it.
Ah the rush of figuring out my fuel.

Astoundingly, my body
knows just what to do with food,
runs reliably on real meals, sluggish
when I won't nourish with care.
My body,
more wise than I imagined
if only I can learn to listen.

The Slip Dress

I've done well for weeks
but want to wear a dress
that is tight

> So tight, you have to fast.

to look good
for an AA wedding.

> *Like a regular wedding*
> *but with recovering alcoholics all joking*
> *everyone will remember it*
> *the next day.*

Black-and-white vertical stripes strain
to stay integrated around my hips.

> Starvation is your only option, pork chop.

I am just   *so hungry.*
Break down over a bag of frozen Ore-Ida!s.
Three shifts in the microwave
salt them up   shove them down
greasy fingers   moving quickly.

Until

> You will never fit that dress
> date will be here in an hour
> you have no choice
> but to flush those
> tots away.

I did it again

> a stupid failure.

Should've known
I can't change.

Sunday Best

I become that misfit chick
in church, sing praises out of tune
smiling, upraised face
I feel so free.

Oh, Lord, you're beautiful
Your face is all I seek
      My attention focused above.
For when your eyes are on this child
Your grace abounds to me
      Hear the screams
      of daddy issues being slaughtered.

But something is so broken
that same face
is staring down the throat
of a yawning toilet bowl
by Tuesday.

That's more like it.

Thursday if it's a good week.

Adventures in String Bean Town

Dad has a friend
with a daughter like me.
She takes me to a group
for anorexics-slash-bulimics
who want to get better.

Held at a hospital
each member
more skeletal than the next
sizing each other up.

There is good healthy discussion,
but talk is cheap
and cannot mask
what is really
The Big Competition.

        Who is thinnest?
        Closest to death?

This one
with a wasted face
or that one
with the thinning hair.

      All skinnier than you.

One girl with big pumpkin cheeks
is so sickly looking
with her spindly limbs
that it is difficult not to admire her.

      Perfect ten across all judges.

She proudly models
hospital scrubs, slippers, bracelet.
So committed she is committed.
She definitely wins,
which is hard on me,

The big loser in the group.
Barely below-average in weight,
hunched over my orange plastic chair
waiting for this pageant to end.

Confessional 2

In the college counseling center
my fingers fidget in my lap
watching the waiting room
floor tiles
preparing what to say.

The blond-bobbed woman
gives me the
saddest eyes
as I confess I'm bulimic
ask her for *help*.

I'm relieved the hard part is over,
but she bites her lined lips
tells me she's
glad I'm ready to get better but
sososorry there's
nothing she can do.
No help here.

My hope,
a bloodied mass on the floor
I drag from her office.
My hope
so tired of struggling
of fighting
of being humiliated,
but   still,
my   hope   breathes.

Solo Performance

My quest for a therapist ends
at the exit.
The college counseling center can't help.
I'm out of ideas.

Turning to books, I try to read *Golden Cage:*
The Enigma of Anorexia Nervosa
by Hilde Bruch, MD, but am not
devastatingly thin   *a failure.*

Twelve steps are great but AA-style meetings
to me, are an Eating Disorder Rodeo,
          stirring me to compete,
                    who can ride that bull hardest?
I can admit I'm powerless, but no way to
abstain from food. For long.

No boyfriend to
ride in on a white horse
    dating paused
    until judgment improves
          according to Mom's book,
    Cinderella Complex,
I have a tendency to
undervalue my worth,
and an unconscious desire
to be rescued.

My happy ending is left up to me.
Guess I'll have to solve this one
    myself.

Stalking Sanity

I scramble and scrabble,
pick myself up, fall
back in. Obsess a little or a lot,
not caring that I'm
starving, bingeing, purging,
choose your form
of self-destruction.

My car harbors
a plastic bag filled
with wrappers and cartons.

You are disgusting.

I can't risk disposing
the garbage at Dad's.

Damning evidence.

I am terrified
of car accidents,
trash from my binges
sitting shotgun beside me.

SPECIAL REPORT
We have a quote from the first responder on the
scene. The officer states, "The car crash was
certainly unfortunate but *WHAT* was with the
overflowing bag of food wrappers we found on the
seat beside the mangled remains of the driver?"
Stay tuned for more disgusting details!

An entire afternoon is spent
at the campus library,
in the tan-tiled bathroom.

Purging plans interrupted,
I'm in a dark corner
death-glaring
a girl as she washes her hands.
Banishing her with laser eyes.

I step forward
from the shadows;
she startles and exits quickly.

How lovely. One more person ~~knowing~~
assuming I'm deranged.
I'm utterly exhausted,
sick about all the time I've
wasted thinking about
what-I-will-eat-or-not-eat-or-what-I-didn't-eat-or-should-eat-
or-worst-of-all-what-I-just-ate.

You ate WHAT?

I call up
my dad's friend's daughter,
the one like me,
ask, "Does anyone
ever recover from this?"
And because she's been

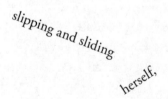

slipping and sliding
herself,

she answers quietly,

"I don't know."

Nightmare 3

I'm so impulsive.
I didn't want to stop, kept going,
shoving it in,
cutting the corner of my mouth
on sharp, salty edge
of a renegade potato chip.

Fitting injury,
disgusting, fat, worthless pigbitch.

I lie awake in the dark.
Aware only
of the food in my body,
the tin taste of my wound, and
that I am

Bad
Bad

Bad
Bad

Bad

Bad

Bad.

Battle Cry

I do not throw up
even though I want to
start fresh   tomorrow.

Don't counterattack.
Surrender my

             Binge
      Starve   Purge
  Guilt   Guilt
      Purge   Starve
             Binge

spinning cycle of futility.
Call for a cease and desist.

Take responsibility.
Sit with it tearfully
as my mind shrieks
What the fuck is wrong with you?
Stupid, disgusting, fat, worthless pigbitch.
~~*You deserve to die*~~

I deserve to live.

I hiss at the thoughts.
"Stop harassing me!"
Earnestly sing Jesus songs out of tune
at the top of my lungs
and with all of my desperate heart.

This little light of mine, I'm gonna let it shine. [[what the fuck?]] *This little light of mine, I'm gonna let it shine.* [[fat, worthless pigbitch]] *This little light of mine, I'm gonna let it shine.* [[you useless whore]] *Let it shine, let it shine, let it shine.* [[fat, worthless pigbitch]] Ha! You said that one already.

I am not going down again
without a fucking *fight.*

Don't Stop Believin'

I choose "eating disorders" as my topic
for a class writing assignment,
hit the library, and
scan through pages of microfiche
reading
• health journals
• magazine articles
• psychology studies
each scrolling across the murky screen
illuminated by a yellowed bulb
as I research
• bulimia nervosa
• anorexia nervosa
• eating disorders not otherwise specified

The language is boring and

an·o·rex·i·a

/anə reksēə/ *noun*

loss of appetite

seems dead wrong because
I am nothing but
appetite.
My mind murmurs at seeing
my symptoms in broad daylight
in plain ten-point font.
My food-thing feels less mine now;
it never made me special,
others share my self-loathing.

Even Princess Diana's been
tossing royal cookies for years,
and comedy queen Gilda Radner,
    who is more majestic
     in my eyes,
claims she's thrown up
in toilets
on every floor
of 30 Rock.

I don't find clear answers,
but continue
studying the evidence.
A name for something
means someone else has done it.

And that means I'm not alone.

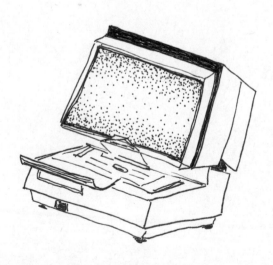

Diseased Culture

Looking back
at all the encouragement
respect
and compliments
I got when
starving myself,
starving my heart,
starving my soul,
it is clear
I am not
the only
sick
one.

Loyalty

I have rejected this body so long
forced myself   outside
so I could observe.
Caring more what others see
than how my body feels.

How can I
  move
    eat
      breathe
    live
  be
from out there?

Cold and tired,
I seek the comfort
of my own flesh
and find
after years of being
  abused
    rejected
      kicked
and abandoned,
my body's still waiting
to forgive
to be loved
waiting
to be invited back inside.

Ex-Lover Encounter

Standing on line at the deli,
my eyes fall to a row of old friends:
orange cakes
their frosted faces
pressed tight on cellophane.

I no longer
imagine they're immoral,
but looking at them
makes me feel dirty.

My mind rolls through
the highlight reel, good times
intoxicating days
before my eating disorder
consumed me.

Picking up a trio,
one-two-three
anxiety rises to my throat,
but I figure *why not*
the sweet trinity hits the counter.

And I'm shocked to discover
when ingested with intention,
my old go-to favorites taste like
I just took a bite
of *The Simpson's* cartoon couch.

Huh?

My Body   gradually finds
its natural size   swings back
and forth   back and forth
like a pendulum   until it settles
at about   where
it was   before
all   this
began.

Which Way to Carnegie Hall?

I practice being at peace with soft curves
before I feel at peace with my soft curves.
Practice not treating gnawing hunger like a victory.
Practice not using food to fill the black void.
Practice being okay taking up space.
Run hands over comfortable roundness.

Practice sitting inside my own skin
when all I want to do is crawl out of it.

Practice forgiving myself,
believing in myself.
Practice *being* myself
before any of it feels natural.

And am amazed
to realize

I am actually
getting better at all of this
with practice.

Generational Curse

Along with ambition
wit and
resilience
I have been *blessed*
with the ample ass of my ancestors.

And so on the dance floor one night
when I'm feeling myself
and the DJ spins a song
celebrating big behinds
then gestures with a wink
toward me and my butt

I take it as a compliment
and swing my heritage to the beat.

Skywriting

I consider
that long lonely plank
where I can feel
better for a time
emotionless
cut off
a trancelike peace
that is not peace.

That hell on a high dive.

In my journal
the dark churning
words and drawings
come up and out in one sour mass.
I write my wounds
until my wrist is sore
and as the dark, festering
basement memories
are unchained,
released,
set loose on paper

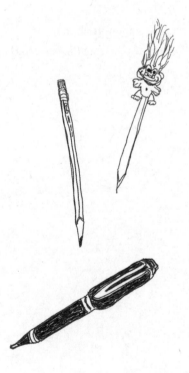

the power they wield
shrivels in the light.

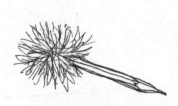

Nature Girl

I am the wanderer,
hiking alone on mountain trails
winding through upstate New York.
Three miles in at Minnewaska State Park,
I'm about to turn back when
the trees part
to a wide-open view
suddenly, I'm breathing sky.

I stand on the edge,
wild hope breath
bringing oxygen to heart that pumps with
Scandalous Faith,
sending blood through veins dangerously
close to my surface,
nearly outside my body;
life tracks
winding through me.

I could fall so far right now

remind myself *relax*.
Run hands down sweaty
cheststomachhips
vessel that carried me here.
Legs, two mighty oaks,
root me to the ground.

I will not fall.

The lake below mirrors sky above
quilt of trees rolled out at my feet

birds swing past
full of life
endlessly celebrating as they
sing in uneven concert, pine incense arises
surrounded by unspeakable beauty

I so want to be a part of it,
and then I realize   I am.

Ohm

Yoga
overlooked
for years
because it
only strengthens
and centers
and teaches me to breathe peace

~~what a waste~~

Cheated
of time
I could have been standing
in Warrior pose.

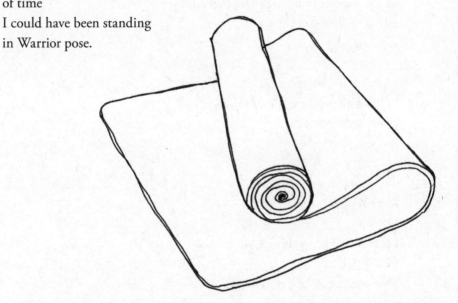

Imposter 5

Channeling my love
of all things *makeup*,
I get a job at ▮▮▮▮, a major department store.
My training
"Your face looks good."
poof "You're a makeup artist."

I write a scathing exposé
of customers getting "the special,"
which consists of telling them everything
they're wearing on their face
is wrong.

I quote one manager's claim,
"This is all just smoke and mirrors.
Give them a show.
Sell this shit."

The article is my first sale
to a national magazine.
Ecstatic,
I tear through the shiny March issue
for my byline.
Discover the piece has been
put through a shredder,
bite and humor and *truth* removed,
so not to offend
the magazine's mighty legion
of cosmetics sponsors.

I want to punch and wail.
  Ahhhhhh! Ahhhhhh! AHHHHHH!
Don't take my voice!

But those fashion magazines
must seek ad sales.
"Give them a show.
Sell this shit."
Readers for sale, are
products neatly packaged,
the more insecure,
the better.

All smoke
and mirrors.

The Bird 2

My body.
And the rest
of the world
can just
flip the fuck off
about it.

Too Sexy for This Store

Hustling through the
supermarket at Columbus Circle,
making my way toward the exit,
I nearly knock over an actual supermodel.
Whose glossy image
I once revered. The face
of magazine covers and music videos,
who has strutted a million miles on catwalks
an iconic beauty
milling about the produce section.

Even without airbrushing, she is
stunning and,

*oh my god, so so
thin.
Am talking like, your
dehydrated corpse
would look chubby next to this woman and—*

STOP!
I push back against the supermodel comparison.
Repeat after me:

**Other womens' bodies
are none of my business.**

The role-model model of my past
doesn't appear any happier
or any less happy than me.
I smile a hello,
and we both sidestep through the crowd
toward our
own   separate destinies.

Mouthful of Cotton

I recline against the red leather
breathing awkwardly
suction straw sipping my spit.
Root canal number nine,
reaping what I've sown.

      Damn stomach acids
      eroding away
      enamel.

I did floss.

Thousands of dollars
and plenty of pain,
the finger of blame
points back at me.

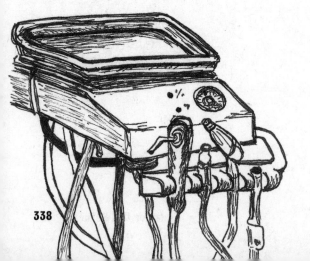

Inner Body Experience

I envision myself as a child
whispering into the thick bark folds
of my favorite tree.
That girl, pure love
radiating outward
and settling delicious on skin.

Mourning the loss of innocence,
I grieve for that child,
so alive, unashamed
before being penetrated
by her culture
lied to about her worth
denied her bodacious power.

Abandoning joy and zeal
to focus on her mirror image.
Brainwashed by some fucked up
mathmatics where the sum
of her attractiveness and her sexuality
equaled her value.

That long-ago girl
endlessly listening for divine whispers
as she skips barefoot
through the grass.
I want to be in that place again.
Not thinking about
how my thighs jiggle when I skip,
just feeling the soft, cool grass
against my bare soles.

Object in Mirror Is Not an Object

At a friend's apartment, I'm
washing up after a loud, shared meal.
  I usually avoid bathrooms
  right after as
  everyone knows my history.
  I don't want to make them wonder.
But I'm with *my* misfits
who've been through their own battles
abandonment, shame, addiction, depression
outpaced their demons,
and we are *all of us*
  battling still,
but we do not war alone. We know we will survive.
  We already have.

We are those reckless, wild ones
who courageously love fragile things
  because everything
  is too fragile when you love it.

I dry my hands
on soft, loose denim-clad thighs,
look up to the glass,
  not checking, just looking,
and there I see her.

Kindness and humor
in clear eyes,
smiling at the private joke–
that we are happy to be together,
alive and free,
worthy of tenderness.

We love each other,
and the punch line
of our favorite inside joke is:
We are so much more
than this mirror can hold.

Epilogue

Liberty Unbound

I decide to change the world
not my size.
Become an activist.
Creating ugly, angry artwork.
I am frustratingly
green and untrained,
feel like I've fallen behind,
missed my chance
to be a *real* artist,
> but I'm passionate
> and there is no such thing
> as too late to remember
we are all artists.
Creating is an act of courage and hope,
and as for me and my art,
pretty is not the point.
> Although *damn* do I wish
> I could draw nice hands.

I deface my bathroom scale, add
A Warning
because a scale can't measure
anyone's sparkling personality.

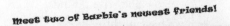

I repurpose fashion dolls into
Anorexia Ana*.
*Accessories include
a pink bathroom scale and
modeling contract!
and **Bulimia Mia***
*with realistic purging action!

Have endless hours of fun helping them up when they faint!
And be sure to collect all of their hair
as it falls out in clumps!

I create bright pink Ms. Yuk stickers
that warn, "Poisonous Image!"
and post them throughout NYC
over ads that glorify starvation.

I run a website dreamer-girl.com
get invited
to present my artwork
at a national eating disorder conference.
I share my story
at churches and high schools and universities.
Give slideshow presentations,
point my finger and shout
"Bullshit!"
to photoshopped images,
impossible standards,
and a wicked diet industry that
runs on the toxic fuel
of all of us hating our bodies,
     feeding the fantasy
       we each need to lose
       approximately ten
       to eighty-five pounds.
As if we have nothing better
to focus on.

Fuck that.

Your body does not need
to be remodeled.

It needs
to be respected,
for the light it holds,
the light you are.

It's a reckless act of rebellion
to love your body
as it is,
to accept every inch,
to celebrate
cellulite, curves,
and all the bouncy bits.
But please
I beg you
do it anyway.

Love yourself.

Your body parts
will not be dissected
from your heart and mind
and inner light. Loving yourself means
loving *all* of yourself.

And oh precious one,
just look now at that torch
in your very own hand.
See its unique brightness.
Do not compare it
or criticize it
or be ashamed
if it seems
not enough
or too weak.

Know that your light
is sacred.
Feel its power burning.
Shining with liberty
and creativity
and life
and youness
and pure love.

Join me,
raise your torch high in the air
and share it with the world.

THE END

RESOURCES

Thankfully, help is much more readily available now than in the late '80s when I was wrestling with my eating disorder. If you or someone you know is struggling in any of the areas mentioned in this book, there is no need to battle alone. Please reach out for help.

Anxiety and Depression

Anxiety and Depression Association of America (https://adaa.org/)
> Find local resources to manage symptoms of depression and anxiety.

National Mental Health Hotline (https://mentalhealthhotline.org/), 1-866-903-3787
> This (noncrisis) hotline provides access to resources related to mental health.

National Suicide and Crisis Lifeline (https://988lifeline.org/), text or call 988
> It offers support for those actively at risk of attempting suicide or self-harm.

Drug and Alcohol Addiction

Alcoholics Anonymous (https://www.aa.org/) or Narcotics Anonymous (https://na.org/)
> Find links to resources or meetings in your area.

American Addiction Centers (https://alcohol.org)
> Read an overview of the condition of alcoholism, plus in-depth discussions.

National Association for Children of Addiction (https://nacoa.org/)
> This advocacy group offers a wide variety of resources for children of alcoholics.

Eating Disorders

Eating Disorder Hope (https://www.eatingdisorderhope.com)
> The site offers up-to-date information and articles on eating disorders and resources for those who wish to recover.

National Association of Anorexia Nervosa and Associated Disorders (https://anad.org)
> Find free peer support groups for people of various backgrounds struggling with eating disorders.

NEDA (https://www.nationaleatingdisorders.org), 1-800-931-2237
> Support, resources, and treatment options are available for those struggling with eating disorders. This number can be called or texted.

Overeaters Anonymous (https://oa.org)
> Find peer support in your area.

Renfrew Center (https://renfrewcenter.com/)
> Eating disorder treatment is available.

Reducing Weight Stigma

National Association to Advance Fat Acceptance (https://naafa.org/)
> This nonprofit wants to protect the rights of and improve the quality of life for overweight people.

Sexual Assault

National Sexual Violence Resource Center (https://www.nsvrc.org/)
    The directory offers help to victims of sexual assault.

Rape, Abuse & Incest National Network (https://rainn.org/), Hotline 1-800-656-4673
    RAINN offers ways to support a loved one who has disclosed their sexual assault.
    The confidential number provides immediate emotional support and ways to
    access long-term psychological, legal, and medical support.

You may also want to check out:

About-Face (https://about-face.org)
    This site has been promoting body acceptance since 1995 and featured early
    links to the author's articles and activist website Dreamer-Girl.com in their
    Gallery of Winners. Dreamer-girl.com has been pared down, but the author can
    occasionally be found slipping Ms Yuck stickers on particularly egregious ads in
    and around NYC.

AdBusters Media Foundation (https://www.adbusters.org/)
    Check out spoof ads at this website by the creators of Buy Nothing Day and
    Kalle Lasn's *Design Anarchy*.

Guerrilla Girls (https://www.guerrillagirls.com)
    These badass anonymous artists use activist art to expose gender and ethnic bias
    and corruption in art, film, politics, and pop culture.

Jean Kilbourne (https://jeankilbourne.com/)
    Jean Kilbourne's pioneering work regarding women and advertising includes her
    classic, eye-opening presentation *Killing Me Softly*.

Bonus Suggestion

Write a poem to your body. And make it a love poem! Or create your own artwork or
essay, slapping back at harmful starvation imagery and the malignant money-hungry
media. Shine your own unique and special and lovely light into the darkness! I'd love
to see what you create! Contact me through my website: Lboylecrompton.com.

Acknowledgments

Grateful shout-out to the best agent ever: Ammi-Joan Paquette, and best editor ever: Shaina Olmanson. I'm so thankful for your skillful help in shaping this book of my heart and ushering it into reader's hands. Special cheers to the teams at EMLA and Lerner. Especially, Erin Murphy, Mariana Montbriand, Danielle Carnito, Athena Currier, Martha Kranes, and Megan Ciskowski. A nod and wink to all my uniquely beautiful fellow misfits who love reckless and wild. You know who you are. To my family of origin who have shared more love, support, and laughter than these pages could possibly capture, youns are all awesome. And to best mate, Brett, and the most precious and entertaining children ever. You three are a dream come true and so worth all the hard work it took to get here. Special gratitude to the Artist, Author, Poet, Musician, and Creator of all. Thanks for *always* being there.

About the Author

Laurie Boyle Crompton is a screenwriter and the author of six young adult novels, including *Pretty in Punxsutawney*, a 2020 ALA Quick Pick for Reluctant Readers. She graduated from St. John's University with a BA in English and journalism, has written for national magazines, survived a teaching stint at an all-boys high school, and appeared on *Good Day New York* as a professional toy expert. Laurie loves speaking to teen and young adult audiences about media awareness and body image in high schools, colleges, and churches. She lives in Queens, New York, with her husband, two children, and three dogs. When she's not writing, Laurie can be found walking barefoot in the grass, biking through the forest or on TV and movie sets in and around NYC where she works as a background artist. She remains committed to spreading the word that advertising sucks and chubby thighs are positively lovely.

The Denim Diaries is Laurie's first nonfiction title.

Text copyright © 2023 by Laurie Boyle Crompton
Images copyright © Laurie Crompton 1998–2023

Zest Books™
An imprint of Lerner Publishing Group, Inc.
241 First Avenue North
Minneapolis, MN 55401 USA

For reading levels and more information, look up this title at www.lernerbooks.com.
Visit us at zestbooks.net. 🇫🇧 🇮🇬

Designed by Athena Currier.
Main body text set in Adobe Garamond Pro.
Typeface provided by Adobe Systems.

Cover: kiwihug/Unsplash; Reddavebatcave/Shutterstock.
Design elements: Marjan Blan/Unsplash; klyaksun/iStock/Getty Images; pashabo/Shutterstock; Julie A. Felton/Shutterstock.

Library of Congress Cataloging-in-Publication Data

Names: Crompton, Laurie Boyle, author.
Title: The denim diaries : a memoir / by Laurie Boyle Crompton.
Description: Minneapolis : Zest Books , 2023. | Audience: Ages 13–18 | Audience: Grades 10–12 | Summary: "From relationships and makeup to divorce and disordered eating, Laurie Boyle Crompton recounts the humor and heartbreak of her coming of age in rural Pennsylvania and New York City during the 1970s and '80s"— Provided by publisher.
Identifiers: LCCN 2023009770 (print) | LCCN 2023009771 (ebook) | ISBN 9781728477503 (library binding) | ISBN 9798765604885 (paperback) | ISBN 9798765602362 (epub)
Subjects: LCSH: Crompton, Laurie Boyle. | Authors, American—21st century—Biography. | LCGFT: Autobiographies. | Autobiographical poetry.
Classification: LCC PS3603.R655 Z46 2023 (print) | LCC PS3603.R655 (ebook) | DDC 811/.6 [B]—dc23/eng/20230307

LC record available at https://lccn.loc.gov/2023009770
LC ebook record available at https://lccn.loc.gov/2023009771

Manufactured in the United States of America
1-52402-50735-8/22/2023